Future of Business and Finance

The Future of Business and Finance book series features professional works aimed at defining, analyzing, and charting the future trends in these fields. The focus is mainly on strategic directions, technological advances, challenges and solutions which may affect the way we do business tomorrow, including the future of sustainability and governance practices. Mainly written by practitioners, consultants and academic thinkers, the books are intended to spark and inform further discussions and developments.

Florian Schnitzhofer

The Self-Driving Company

A Conceptual Model for Organizations of the Future

Florian Schnitzhofer
Linz, Austria

ISSN 2662-2467 ISSN 2662-2475 (electronic)
Future of Business and Finance
ISBN 978-3-662-68147-3 ISBN 978-3-662-68148-0 (eBook)
https://doi.org/10.1007/978-3-662-68148-0

© The Editor(s) (if applicable) and The Author(s), under exclusive license to Springer-Verlag GmbH, DE, part of Springer Nature 2023

This work is subject to copyright. All rights are solely and exclusively licensed by the Publisher, whether the whole or part of the material is concerned, specifically the rights of translation, reprinting, reuse of illustrations, recitation, broadcasting, reproduction on microfilms or in any other physical way, and transmission or information storage and retrieval, electronic adaptation, computer software, or by similar or dissimilar methodology now known or hereafter developed.

The use of general descriptive names, registered names, trademarks, service marks, etc. in this publication does not imply, even in the absence of a specific statement, that such names are exempt from the relevant protective laws and regulations and therefore free for general use.

The publisher, the authors, and the editors are safe to assume that the advice and information in this book are believed to be true and accurate at the date of publication. Neither the publisher nor the authors or the editors give a warranty, expressed or implied, with respect to the material contained herein or for any errors or omissions that may have been made. The publisher remains neutral with regard to jurisdictional claims in published maps and institutional affiliations.

This Springer imprint is published by the registered company Springer-Verlag GmbH, DE, part of Springer Nature.
The registered company address is: Heidelberger Platz 3, 14197 Berlin, Germany

Paper in this product is recyclable.

Preface

I have been involved with the self-driving company, both as a vision and as a blueprint, my entire life. In working with top European companies, this vision has reached a level of clarity and detail that it can form the basis of this book. I would like to share my vision with readers and, depending on their own interests and needs, highlight the many opportunities it presents. With the self-driving company, I would like to provide an economics-based direction that economy and society can take in their further development. All decision makers, entrepreneurs, and politicians should be encouraged to adopt those aspects of the blueprint of relevance to them, enabling them to implement those steps that will be decisive for their organizations and companies in the next 10–15 years.

Linz, Austria   Florian Schnitzhofer

Acknowledgments

I would like to express my heartfelt thanks to all my ReqPOOL colleagues, friends, and family with whom I had good discussions, conversations, and in-depth exchanges on the vision of the self-driving company. In particular, I would like to mention the following individuals:

- Philipp Ambros
- Christian Buchegger
- Martin Lenz
- Patrick Pils
- Achim Röhe
- Peter Schnitzhofer
- Jakob Strasser
- Andreas Viehhauser

I would like to thank Natalie Hutterer for providing graphic illustration of the contents in this book.

Special thanks go to my devoted editor, Dr. Bernhard Ulrich, who was a very great support to me in the writing of this book.

I would like to give my biggest thanks to Neil Solomon for the great translation into English.

Contents

1	**Introduction**	1
2	**The Vision**	3
	2.1 The Company of 2035	3
	2.1.1 Autonomy	4
	2.1.2 Sustainability	5
	2.1.3 Humanity	5
	2.1.4 Resilience	5
	2.2 The Path to the Self-Driving Company	6
	2.2.1 Levels of Autonomy	7
	2.2.2 The Analog Company	7
	2.2.3 Level 1: The Digital Company	8
	2.2.4 Level 2: Partially Automated Business Operations	8
	2.2.5 Level 3: Fully Automated Business Operations	8
	2.2.6 Level 4: The Self-Driving Company	8
	2.3 The Victory of Algorithms and the End of Processes	9
	2.4 New Forms of Organization: The Anti-Hierarchy	11
	2.4.1 The Organization from a Theoretical Perspective	11
	2.4.2 The Transformation to an Agile Organization	12
	2.4.3 Departments and Hierarchies Are Dissolved	12
	2.4.4 Improving Working Conditions	14
	2.4.5 The Two Benefits Available to Coworkers	14
	2.5 Software, Algorithms, and Artificial Intelligence	16
	2.5.1 What Is an Algorithm?	17
	2.5.2 Artificial Intelligence for Decision Makers	18
	2.5.3 Neural Networks and Deep Learning	23
	2.5.4 Application Areas for Artificial Intelligence	25
	2.5.5 Requirements for Intelligent Algorithms	26
	2.6 What Comes After Industry 4.0 and Digitization?	28
	2.7 Why Software-Driven Companies?	30
	2.7.1 Cost Effects and Marginal Effects	33
	2.7.2 Effects on Different Roles	34

	2.7.3	Subjectively Perceived Threats from Self-Driving Companies	34
	2.7.4	When Is a Company Considered Self-Driving?	35
	2.7.5	The Seven Central Propositions	36
2.8	Guidelines for Evolution		37
References			42

3 GRANOBIZ: An Example from 2035 45
Reference 51

4 Digitization and Technical Word Bingo 53
4.1	Setup of Complex Software Projects		56
	4.1.1	Comparative Estimates	56
	4.1.2	Expert Estimates	57
	4.1.3	Estimates Made by the Development Team	57
4.2	The Monolithic Heart: Enterprise Resource Planning		57
4.3	The Customer Is King: Customer Relationship Management		60
4.4	Automation Through Software Robots		62
4.5	The Architecture of Company Software		64

5 Problem Areas in Analog Companies 67
5.1	The Classic Company		68
5.2	Interaction with the Market and Customers		70
	5.2.1	Helpdesk and Customer Hotline	71
5.3	Value-Adding Processes, Logistics, and Production		72
	5.3.1	From the Idea to the Product	72
	5.3.2	From Forecast to Customer Delivery	73
5.4	Interaction with Partners and Suppliers		74
5.5	Finance and Accounting—and Corporate Management		75
	5.5.1	From Record to Report	76
	5.5.2	From Strategy to Management	77
5.6	Organization and Personnel		80
	5.6.1	From Personnel Planning to Recruiting	80
	5.6.2	From Investment to Divestment	81
	5.6.3	Facility Management	82
References			83

6 The Self-Driving Company 85
6.1	Interaction with Market and Customers		85
	6.1.1	Growth Hacking Instead of Marketing	88
	6.1.2	Example: The Analog and Digital Furniture Retailer	90
	6.1.3	Example: Supermarket Scenarios	92
	6.1.4	The Future Shape of Retailing	95
6.2	Interaction with Partners and Suppliers		96
6.3	Value Creation in the Self-Driving Organization		99
	6.3.1	Research and Development	100

		6.3.2 Production Forecasting and Planning	102
		6.3.3 Automation of Production	102
		6.3.4 Robotics and Digital Twins	104
		6.3.5 Automated Storage	104
	6.4	Finance and Accounting and Corporate Management	106
		6.4.1 Interaction with the State and the Reinvention of Taxes	107
		6.4.2 A Day in the Life of a Manager in 2035	110
		6.4.3 Leadership in the Self-Driving Organization	111
	6.5	Organization and Personnel	112
		6.5.1 Self-Organizing Teams	113
		6.5.2 Software-Driven Teams	116
		6.5.3 Matching and the Hunt for Key Workers	117
	References		118
7	**Humans and the Self-Driving Organization**		119
	7.1	Six Theses on the Role of Humans in Companies in 2035	120
	7.2	An Example of Defensiveness: The Self-Driving Train	121
	7.3	Employees and Their Life Cycle in the Self-Driving Organization	121
		7.3.1 The Role of Leadership	123
		7.3.2 The Role of Management	123
		7.3.3 The Role of Knowledge Workers	124
		7.3.4 The Role of Workers	124
		7.3.5 The Role of Auxiliary Workers	125
	7.4	Who "Is" the Self-Driving Company?	126
	7.5	The Self-Driving Company: By People for People	126

About the Author

Florian Schnitzhofer is a visionary and management consultant for software, owner of the ReqPOOL Group, and investor in highly scalable AI software companies. He advises the top management of leading companies in Germany and Austria on the most important topics related to digital transformation and intelligent software solutions. As a graduate computer scientist, Mr. Schnitzhofer founded numerous software and consulting companies in Germany and Austria and passes on his experience and knowledge in university courses and lectures. With his vision of the self-driving company, Mr. Schnitzhofer wants to revolutionize the way in which companies create value and how they are organized.

Introduction

1

Throughout the history of mankind, it has been shown time and again that everything that was technically possible and useful was eventually put into practice. This development extended over thousands of years from the invention of the wheel to the steam engine, the automobile, and the personal computer. Those peoples, and later companies, which successfully adopted these technologies have always gained enormous advantages.

Today, we stand at a new threshold of technological evolution. The global networking of data and the use of artificial intelligence are creating unprecedented potential opportunities for companies. Those who have already recognized this potential are now among the top players and are generating unbelievable profits with astonishingly modest resources. Most companies, however, are still stuck at a level of development found at the turn of the millennium. With outdated systems, they try to cope with the exponentially accelerating transformation of their increasingly global environment. They are focusing enormous forces on increasingly short-term tactical moves. As a result, they are losing sight of a promising future.

This book with its depiction of the self-driving company seeks to produce an economic blueprint and a realistic vision of the future. All boring routines and processes come under the control of software, freeing up people for creative and empathetic activities. All functions in the company are networked in real time with each other and with their relevant environment. This results in a superorganism, which is aligned with all the cells in the company in pursuit of a clear goal. This self-driving company adapts to new requirements in a holistically automated way, learning continuously, never losing focus, never tiring, and knowing at all times the state of each and every organ of its agile organism. The technical basis for this already exists today. It is therefore a matter of obtaining a clear picture of the goal and a blueprint. Then one can prepare the way to get there, something that is described in the following chapters in a practical manner, using numerous examples.

© The Author(s), under exclusive license to Springer-Verlag GmbH, DE, part of Springer Nature 2023
F. Schnitzhofer, *The Self-Driving Company*, Future of Business and Finance, https://doi.org/10.1007/978-3-662-68148-0_1

The Vision

2

The idea that companies will develop into self-driving organizations has not yet become a topic of public discourse. There is extensive discussion of the ubiquitous digitization taking place, but there is currently no vision of a destination that goes beyond short-term developments. From individual developments, such as artificial intelligence and self-driving cars, a rather blurry picture may be emerging of what these developments could mean for our companies. One thing is certain: the successful ones will be quicker to seize these opportunities; they already have an idea of the enormous potential that will result from these technological advances.

In order to open up these opportunities to everyone else, it is the goal of this book to create a clear, attractive, and fascinating picture of the future that will result from this technological progress. As software strategy consultants to major corporations, we know that self-driving companies will emerge. We know the crucial steps to get there and can also provide very good estimates of the accompanying measures. For us, the self-driving company of 2035 is no longer just a vision, but an outcome that will be achieved by all those who take the necessary measures now. So what does this vision of our future, this outcome, look like?

2.1 The Company of 2035

The self-driving company will be part of our reality in just a few years and it is important to think through this vision in advance. The focus is not on the current change project or the goals of the 5-year strategy. The vision goes much further and involves four elementary dimensions: autonomy, sustainability, resilience, and humanity (see Fig. 2.1). Each of these dimensions contributes decisively to the success of the self-driving company.

© The Author(s), under exclusive license to Springer-Verlag GmbH, DE, part of Springer Nature 2023
F. Schnitzhofer, *The Self-Driving Company*, Future of Business and Finance,
https://doi.org/10.1007/978-3-662-68148-0_2

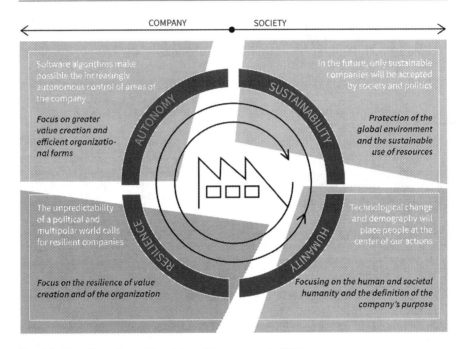

Fig. 2.1 Four dimensions of the vision of the company in 2035

2.1.1 Autonomy

This is the central starting point from which all further findings result: The enterprise of 2035 will act largely autonomously. Many decisions will no longer be made by humans, but by artificial intelligence. Our current problem is based on a lack of knowledge and the uncertainty that results from it: for largely irrational reasons, we shy away from actively addressing the opportunities that artificial intelligence (AI) presents our company with.

The reason for this is not only irrational, but also highly emotional: for many people, AI has negative connotations, which again is primarily due to a lack of knowledge. We may already be using the Google translator or voice-to-text input, but we don't seem to know that we are using high-performance AI from Silicon Valley here. Those who have already realized this are thus somewhat more positive about this development. Now we know that AI can replace a multilingual secretary. More of the completely autonomous company only comes into view once we add other aspects to the picture.

2.1.2 Sustainability

Sustainability is already a much-discussed topic. Nonsustainable companies are viewed as increasingly less acceptable, especially among millennials. By 2035 the latter will make up a significant proportion of all economic actors. It is argued here that an autonomous company in 2035 must be sustainable without exception, and must operate accordingly.

Why is this more possible with a self-driving company than with a company where all decisions are made by humans? Because people make short-term decisions and are unable to consider all the long-term aspects of any given decision. In the firm belief that they are thinking rationally, important aspects of sustainability are missed. The self-driving company is like an organism that is fully networked internally and externally, constantly calculating all scenarios based on all data. Even today, artificial intelligence is already far superior to us in many areas. In 2035, it will ensure sustainability in terms of both corporate success as well as overriding ecological and economic goals.

2.1.3 Humanity

Although the company of 2035 will act largely autonomously, its focus will nonetheless be on people in every respect. The fear that computers could gain control over people is completely unfounded. They have no motives and no will of their own. In 2035, they will continue to do exactly what we have programmed them to do. The difference between now and then is that they will continue to learn at an incredible rate. But the direction will always be set by humans.

We can embark on this adventure in a positive frame of mind because we will be able to accurately assess the consequences of every step along the way: for we will always have all the facts and figures at our disposal in real time and with an unprecedented degree of transparency. With all operational and tactical decisions being made by the system, people will have their heads free to think about and improve upon humanitarian concerns.

However, the company of 2035 must not only be human-oriented, it must also be humanitarian. For instance, any form of human exploitation already comes in for strong criticism today and will be even less acceptable in the future. Again, the reason for this lies in transparency: it will no longer be possible to conceal unfavorable practices in the self-driving company. The markets will be open only to those companies that strictly adhere to humanitarian principles.

2.1.4 Resilience

The period following the end of the Cold War has shown: the world is becoming more uncertain, or at least more unpredictable. This is reflected in the fact that many companies are hardly able to plan ahead for the medium term. But this trouble with medium-term strategic goals obscures the view of the big vision, the self-driving company of 2035.

In the fully networked company, the extensive real-time data available will ensure extreme agility and robustness: These companies will be resilient. In other words, they will function even under adverse conditions, e.g., in economic crises or in a pandemic. Forward-looking planning and projections of real-time data enable resilient management of companies; risks are identified early and can be largely mitigated with the help of simulations.

2.2 The Path to the Self-Driving Company

The reason why the path to the self-driving company is already beginning today is based first of all on growing complexity. This is felt not only in our everyday lives, but is also making it increasingly difficult for companies to act: ever more competition, global sales and procurement markets, ever more customer data, greater product diversity, more individualized services, and much more.

This increasing complexity can and must be mastered in the future. This requires the use of self-learning algorithms. With the increasing global networking of all devices and individuals and the resulting exponential increase in the amount of data, we are already reaching the limit of what can be humanly managed.

According to a study by the International Data Corporation (cited in Statista, 2021), alone the data volume of 33 zettabytes in 2018 will more than quintuple to 175 zettabytes by 2025, which is 175,000,000,000,000,000,000 bytes. The key problem for businesses is not storing these extreme amounts of data, but actively using them.

Only with artificial intelligence can we once again make this complexity manageable and remain the decision-makers. That is why more and more companies are looking at these new possibilities. In interaction with the volume of data, there is a further catalyst for this trend, which has already been ongoing for years: the rapid continued development of our computer systems and the increased use of software algorithms. This enables the increasingly autonomous management of more and more areas or functions in the company—in part completely autonomously, in part hand in hand with humans.

Whereas in the past the main tasks of our computer systems were to collect, store, and process our data, in the future algorithms will make intelligent decisions based on our data and execute them autonomously—much faster and more precisely than we humans could. The tasks of humans will focus on the specification of strategies, the development of creative approaches for solving problems, and interpersonal interaction. Routine and repetitive tasks in particular will be performed by mechatronic robotic systems and intelligent software systems.

2.2.1 Levels of Autonomy

The transition to a self-driving company is comparable to the development of self-driving vehicles. This is why this term was chosen, as it is easier to imagine and, in this way, provides greater clarity to the vision. The technical maturity of the self-driving, or—semantically correct—the "self-adapting" company can be illustrated using the autonomy levels depicted in Fig. 2.2, which also serve as guidelines for autonomous driving vehicles.

The goal of the evolution to the self-driving company is the further development of all company areas from the analog to the highest level of autonomy. Along the way, individual teams, departments, and divisions will evolve at different speeds. As a result, different areas in the company will move at different levels of autonomy. Only when the majority of all areas have completely transformed themselves can we speak of a self-driving company. The following sections describe these levels of evolution or autonomy and their significance for teams, processes, and results.

2.2.2 The Analog Company

All companies that have evolved historically started this technical transformation as analog companies. Around the turn of the millennium, many companies were already able to "digitize" parts of their organization. Digital media were used instead of paper. And instead of letters and faxes, emails were sent and documents were created digitally on a PC. Nevertheless, these processes are referred to as "analog" because the data were not stored in a way that could be understood by software algorithms. An incoming invoice serves as an example. This is scanned at the receiving end, but then forwarded to the recipient as a PDF or image attached to an email. The content and purpose of this image remains hidden from the software algorithm, and the processing procedure is identical to that of a paper-based process.

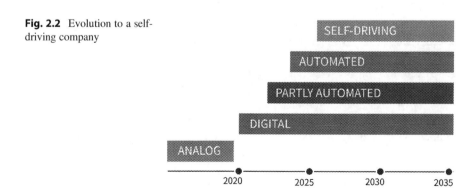

Fig. 2.2 Evolution to a self-driving company

2.2.3 Level 1: The Digital Company

The basis for digital companies is the existence of all data in fully digital form. This data can be read by software algorithms and its content can be understood. Mechatronic robots, software systems, or external platforms use this data foundation and contribute to value creation. The technical systems and algorithms assist with all corporate tasks—and not just with parts of the core processes, as is the case in most companies today.

The planning work and the strategic, tactical, and operational decision-making authority still lie with the human workforce. Integrated software systems evaluate company data across the board and propose recommendations for action for any decisions to be made.

2.2.4 Level 2: Partially Automated Business Operations

In partially automated business operations, integrated software solutions already take over the independent planning and intelligent execution of individual transactional tasks. These clearly defined individual tasks are monitored and managed by means of human interaction. At level 2, the entire company continues to be based on the cooperation of technology and human labor.

2.2.5 Level 3: Fully Automated Business Operations

In companies at this level and above, software solutions already take over a large part of business execution, and processes are fully automated. The software makes programmed decisions and, in most cases, implements them according to the given specifications and strategy.

Unexpected exceptions and complex decisions or tasks are still executed manually. The human workforce is controlled by software solutions and supports automated business implementation. Management, planning, and control of the business remain manual processes.

2.2.6 Level 4: The Self-Driving Company

A self-driving company is defined as a highly automated, self-controlling, and goal-implementing enterprise in all of its existing business domains. By definition, the majority of decisions in self-driving companies are made by intelligent software algorithms. Only rare and exceptional cases still need to be implemented manually. Human interaction is scheduled for empathic, creative, and strategic activities in an automated way. Planned business success is achieved through fully automated processes. The company reacts holistically, intelligently, quickly, and precisely to changing market conditions. It adapts autonomously to changing external and internal conditions within the framework of its strategic guidelines. Employees are recruited automatically, and democratic voting processes ensure fit with the corporate culture. Partner companies are automated and contracted according to forecasted demand, and value creation and administration are handled by software-driven autonomous functions.

The company's management and shareholders configure and program its strategic requirements and framework. They decide on the basis of simulations of future business. The latter allow them to see with maximum transparency whether the strategic specifications make sense and can be implemented on the basis of all available, highly up-to-date data.

2.3 The Victory of Algorithms and the End of Processes

First, end-to-end processes are digitized and automated. The use of intelligent, self-learning algorithms ultimately results in the "destruction" of these processes. A fully networked overall organism emerges, whose former processes become partial software systems that communicate with each other continuously and in real time and share their system status with each other. The former, comparatively rigid, linear process with a starting and ending point then becomes history. This will also change thinking in the company—away from linear thinking from the beginning to the end of a process and within the bounds of a department—toward holistic networked thinking. The information for this will be continuously provided by the software, although this will only be the relevant or explicitly desired information, since almost all decisions will be made by the software itself. The evolution from processes to algorithms proceeds along the same lines as the evolution to the self-driving company. Digitization prepares the data for algorithmic processing. Thereafter, processes are programmed, as a rule, to run completely automatically. The final evolutionary stage is the replacement of linear processes and then even automated ones with intelligently networked and thinking software systems.

In accordance with the motto "Algorithms are the bosses and data is the currency," the structures in companies will change fundamentally. Algorithms will replace all processes and thus enable real-time networking of all operational functions, creating a multidimensional organism.

A typical example of a process in the classic "analog" company is the principle of double verification required for approving payments, for instance, a hospitality voucher for 1000 €, which begins with the review of the receipt, followed by an evaluation of the service rendered, and finally ends with the rele€ase of payment. In the corresponding algorithm of the self-driving company, the receipt itself as well as all associated data is available in electronic, machine-readable form. The programmed, rule- and AI-based algorithms make an immediate decision and trigger the appropriate actions, which are handled by all follow-on algorithms (authorization of payment, booking, liquidity planning, ongoing project calculation, simulation of currently relevant scenarios, and so on).

Since the definition of the self-driving company is based on automated decisions, it is worth going deeper into the topic of decision making. Software algorithms make decisions differently than a human would. They calculate correlations from large amounts of data, which are then perceived as decisions. Human decisions, on the other hand, are made in the form of a value-based, intuitive deliberation process even when the factual basis is thin.

In addition, it is important to understand that artificial intelligence algorithms do not make decisions on their own: instead, human programmers have in fact predefined the desired scope for decision-making. In technical terms, this is done via general threshold values and defined outcome parameters, which then enable a decision to be made in an individual case. In effect, the programmers of the algorithm make a meta-decision that provides a rough guideline for all individual decisions. How learning algorithms work is described in detail in Sect. 2.5.

For artificial intelligence algorithms there is a direct connection between "making decisions" and "making mistakes." The basis for meaningful learning and making correct decisions is making and recognizing mistakes. Learning algorithms gather a large amount of input data, following in this way the programmed software flow. In the process of making decisions, errors often occur at the beginning. Humans or other algorithms detect these errors and report them back to the algorithm. By means of this feedback loop, intelligent algorithms learn. Based on the reported error, they correct their decision parameters and the changed configuration is already the basis for the next decision process. By detecting errors, the algorithm learns and adapts retroactively so that it does not make the same mistake a second time. This is the basic principle of the unsupervised, self-learning algorithm and explains why algorithms need to be trained at the beginning. It is also at the root of the problem that after a period of active learning, the algorithmic decision is no longer comprehensible to humans in individual cases. Especially in self-learning algorithms, the decision behavior of the algorithm changes on the basis of the errors reported back to it. In the next 5–10 years, we will increasingly train these learning algorithms for the individual special cases in our companies, and they will perform these tasks with a high degree of perfection. The next step will then be for the algorithms to interact with each other based on the available data and form a decision network that extends throughout the company.

As a result, the AI-based company will operate in a completely new dimension, far from the old end-to-end processes: faster, more accurate, more versatile, and more cost-effective. The way owners and top managers think will change fundamentally. Companies will be structured completely differently: the classic organizational charts and hierarchies of the organizational structure will give way to functions, boundaries within departments will be dissolved, as will boundaries to partners and suppliers. The transformation will be greater than all the previous stages of the four technical revolutions. It is not just based on more powerful processors, more memory, better laptops, networks, and selective use of artificial intelligence. The huge leverage comes from the fact that everything is fully integrated for the first time in history. The gain in productivity results from this comprehensive transformation.

This also increases, to an extreme degree, the ability of the company as a whole to align all of its decisions according to an overall optimum. Anyone who has worked in a larger, hierarchically structured organization for a longer period of time knows that, over time, each department develops its own systems logic and, above all, lines its own pockets in order to gain relative advantages over other departments. Information is withheld, errors are covered up, or false data is passed on, causing considerable damage over a long period of time without being noticed—often this only becomes apparent when the people concerned have long since left the company. With the self-driving company, this will no longer be possible; complete transparency will lead to a change in behavior, as any misconduct will be identified immediately. However, this does not mean that people are now driven willy-nilly by the system. Instead, they will be mentally freed up to devote themselves to the really interesting tasks found outside of the continuously repeated routines and processes.

2.4 New Forms of Organization: The Anti-Hierarchy

Many organizations face the challenge of responding to changes in the marketplace, new technologies, growing competition from startups, individual customer needs, and a lack of human resources. They are constantly subjected to internal and external influences and changes. The speed of change is also increasing due to globalization and technologization.

In classic, hierarchically structured forms of organization, the poorly networked technical departments are often unable to keep up with this speed due to the way they work—which means that the potential of agile development cannot be exploited. With "agile" software and equally agile organizational forms, it becomes possible to quickly adapt and further develop products and other corporate functions to these changes. The decisive factor here is that decisions and tasks are assigned and performed decentrally. This great advantage of agile organizations ensures that everyone is pursuing the same goal. In order for this decentralization to be successfully implemented, a framework must first be created.

2.4.1 The Organization from a Theoretical Perspective

Organizations form a framework for a system in which resources can be used to achieve organizational goals. These resources must be coordinated to produce high output. In doing so, the tasks of those involved must be specified, coordinated, and checked. With these specifications, complexity is reduced. It is crucial for the efficient use of resources to ensure that all participants pursue common goals. The success of companies therefore depends on the "cooperation" of resources—on how concertedly people and technology are deployed in the individual areas to achieve the overriding goals. While this is already a difficult task for fixed frameworks, it poses a challenge of the highest complexity when changes are ongoing. However, this adaptability of organizations is more crucial than ever for their existence and success.

2.4.2 The Transformation to an Agile Organization

The transformation to an agile organization can be well illustrated by the example of a software company. By focusing on the expectations of customers or markets, companies are evolving from IT service providers to digital solution providers. The perspective that is thus adopted here is not that of the manufacturer's product but that of the user's needs, and the latter must be responded to in an agile manner.

With regard to the organization of this agile company, a vertical product cut is a prerequisite. Digital products are no longer cut horizontally. In classically horizontal organizations, there were breaks between the organizational units, such as between the data center and the development department. A vertical product cut allows products and services to be viewed and managed holistically. The coordinating task is performed by product managers who are networked with all relevant players in the company. From identifying customer needs to developing prototypes, from testing, operation, lifecycle management and growth hacking (see Sect. 6.1.1), all tasks relating to the product are handled by the product manager's team.

In classic organizations, on the other hand, there is a separate team for each task, for example, a sales manager who captures the needs of the market, a research and development department, and a marketing and PR department, each of which tends to develop its own goals and pursue its own interests. Thus, traditional organizations lack a holistic perspective and a shared vision for the product.

Bringing all of these tasks together into one team comes with the introduction of Business, Development & IT Operations (BizDevOps). These interdisciplinary teams make it possible—on the basis of a digital transformation—to generate significant economic benefits for the entire company.

In the software company example above, the transformation from service provider to solution provider takes place. The introduction of a vertical product cut requires a radical change in the organizational form. Because responsibility for entire products is now borne by teams, the decision-making authority must also lie here. This decentralized structure significantly accelerates the speed of development and adaptation. There are various agile organizational models, which differ in their areas of application and in their administrative overhead. Agility must always be introduced at all levels of the organization. Accordingly, the agile working approach must also encompass the corporate management level.

2.4.3 Departments and Hierarchies Are Dissolved

Business and IT expertise are brought together in each team. These interdisciplinary "business informatics specialists" become the drivers of digital transformation. In practice, it has proven effective to make new hires for this purpose. It has been

2.4 New Forms of Organization: The Anti-Hierarchy

shown that it is not worthwhile to retrain "old-established" boomers whose thinking has been shaped by decades in classic structures. In their place, digital natives must assume these positions for the transformation phase to an agile company.

The "old" management will be abolished; only charismatic "leaders" will remain. They lead by communicating their vision in a motivating and authentic way and by acting as role models. The "Excel" management (middle management) will be replaced in the next 5–10 years, as algorithms do these tasks better and faster via self-learning. Instead of the classic hierarchical organization with clearly defined departments, multidimensionally networked, self-managing teams will be established. The management of these self-guiding teams is based on objectives and key results (OKR), which serve as guiding motivation.

OKR is primarily about excellence in implementation. The objective sets the direction and the measurable key results prove success or nonsuccess. This system of objectives is suitable for entire companies, individual teams, as well as individual employees. The objectives must be inspiring and motivating. To achieve this, it must be possible to answer the question "Why?" Ambition and passion can only be ignited in people if there is a clear and convincing idea of purpose. Goals are meaningful, they are action-oriented, they are inspiring. Even rock star Bono of the Irish band U2 has used OKRs for years to fight poverty and disease on a global scale. With the One organization, he has focused on two major goals for the world's poorest countries: debt relief and free access to anti-HIV drugs.

After "Why" comes the question of "How" to achieve key results. In 1999, John Doerr demonstrated the OKR system to Google's co-founders, Larry Page and Sergey Brin, while they were working in their garage at the age of 24. Sergey was excited about it and wanted to apply it, even in the adverse circumstances given, so he decided, "we don't have any other way . . ., so we'll give it a go." Since then, each Google employee defines his or her key results on a quarterly basis. These are evaluated and published, and everyone in the company can see them. All key results serve a common, higher purpose: "Organize the world's information and make it universally accessible and usable" (Doerr, 2018). In addition to these world-changing goals—ending global poverty or accessing all of the world's information—goals that possess high motivational power can also be defined for any other domain.

While the management of teams in agile organizations is taken on by charismatic individuals, algorithms and software such as *Atlassian Jira* guide the coordination of these teams. For this purpose, management interfaces have to be created. Task and requirements catalogs are created and reported via so-called "backlogs." In turn, a product manager takes these and prepares them for his or her team. The "scrum master" handles problems and the operational and tactical management of the team. Via the central software management body, it is thus ensured in an automated way during ongoing operations that all teams are focused on the major objective or objectives they share. Subsequently, artificial intelligence will allow this software to become increasingly smarter.

2.4.4 Improving Working Conditions

A significant advantage of self-driving companies is the elimination of inhumane working conditions. A particularly relevant example of this are the legions of employees who spend all day peering into their PCs to pull out and prepare reports and analyses using Excel. Since humans are creatures of habit, many people have become accustomed over the years to this basically completely mindless work and can no longer imagine doing anything else. They have blocked out or already forgotten how diverse the possibilities of human feeling, thinking, and acting are. How to master exciting challenges together in teams, how to solve problems holistically, taking into account all aspects of economy, ecology, and ethics for the benefit of all people. These "Excel employees" will not think about these aspects in their monotonous, yet demanding and tiring work. They will simply stubbornly implement whatever they are given from above in order to achieve certain numerical targets. This also leads us to realize that the state of our world in terms of climate crisis, pollution, and exploitation is based on this form of inhumane work. As research clearly demonstrates, top executives often possess narcissistic personalities without capacity for empathy and pursue only corporate goals with a very narrow focus. With the Excel wage slaves, you get compliant objects willing to satisfy their desires. With the self-driving company, there is justified hope that people will be relieved of these completely one-sided routines, for which a 286 Intel computer was already able to provide enough computing power in 1982.

2.4.5 The Two Benefits Available to Coworkers

In this context, we deliberately speak of "coworkers" or "associates" as the role of those who were formerly employees will change significantly by 2035 (more on this in Sect. 6.5).

The productivity gain of self-driving companies comes at the right time in recent human history. Due to demographic changes in Western society, we will have significantly fewer workers available in 2035. Increased productivity will allow future coworkers in self-driving companies to choose between two models:

1. Coworkers who enjoy higher salaries due to productivity gains
2. Coworkers who enjoy more free time with high salaries due to productivity gains

Coworkers will be free to choose one of the two options as far as their personal situation allows.

A clear change in values was already evident among the younger generations in 2020, the so-called Millennials and Generation Z. In contrast to previous generations of the workforce, they do not want to devote their entire lives exclusively to their careers. They are interested to a much greater extent in a balance between leisure and work and pursue instead diverse forms of self-realization. While the issue of security played a central role for older generations, it is natural for these younger generations

2.4 New Forms of Organization: The Anti-Hierarchy

and future ones as well to continue their education throughout their lives and to continually take on new challenges.

Model 1 is particularly interesting for those for whom income continues to play a major role or who are in a phase of life, for instance, in which they have to cope with high expenses in connection with the purchase of residential property. Model 2 will meet the needs of the majority of future coworkers. They appreciate the opportunity to continuously improve their qualifications and thus generate an ever higher income combined with less working time. This means that they no longer have to spend 50 h with the same routines and without prospects for the future in the company. It is no longer a matter of doing time in the company and looking at the clock every 10 min to see how one's own valuable time is slipping away. This is a practice that has unfortunately been widespread and rarely questioned for decades. Rather, as already mentioned, the focus will be on creative and interpersonal activities. Especially in creative activities, the place where the work is done as well as the point in time is less relevant.

This was already recognized in the 1980s by the famous creative talent Walter Lürzer, later editor of the journal *Lürzer's Archive*, in which the world's best creative advertising campaigns were published. While still employed as a creative director at a Frankfurt agency, he returned late from an extended lunchtime walk. When his boss reprimanded him for this in the elevator—Lürzer replied: "What do you actually pay me for? For my head or my ass?" (Schönert, 1996).

Increasingly creative activities will free people up to perform at their best when they are at their best. Everyone knows the agonizing hours between 2 and 4 p.m. when basically nothing gets done and it would be better to play sports outdoors, drink coffee in the shade of a lime tree, or play with your children. This typical performance curve also explains the fact that part-time employees in most professions perform about 80% of the workload of full-time employees in half a day. Applied to the new work situation of people in the self-driving company of 2035, this means that only 5–6 h of work per day are actually required to match the full workload of previous employees. In fact, this workload will be far surpassed in terms of quality: the content of the work will be considerably upgraded because routine tasks will be taken over by systems.

Creativity does not arise under stress in a cramped office, but above all when, after intensive discussion, a sense of detachment from the problem is achieved, while taking a walk, in the shower, or in the bathtub, as evidenced by the story of Archimedes: The Greek mathematician was commissioned by King Hiero II of Syracuse to determine whether the crown he had made for himself was really made of gold. Archimedes was thus confronted with a previously unsolved and complex problem. He did not know how to go about it, given the difficult geometry of the crown. When Archimedes climbed into an overfull bathtub at home and it overflowed, he had discovered the principle of buoyancy (hydrostatics)—and the solution to his problem came over him like a flash of inspiration: You need a comparative or reference unit of the same weight as the crown. If the crown is made of pure gold and not an alloy, for example, it will displace just as much water as the comparative or reference mass of pure gold. If the crown displaces more water, it has a larger volume and therefore a lower weight than the same volume of pure gold. After this realization Archimedes is said to have run naked through the streets for joy, oblivious to one and all. So if people are fully committed to a task, they will not switch off their brains upon leaving company grounds. They will happily and easily allow ideas to "bubble up" if conditions are right, and they will bring these ideas back into the company.

It is easy to imagine and scientifically substantiated for decades how, under previous working conditions, motivation was purely extrinsic, that is, based on rewards and punishments. The real and lasting form of motivation, intrinsic motivation, passionate involvement with the matter at hand for its own sake, was found by people in their hobbies if at all. Time and again, plant managers were annoyed observing sluggish workers suddenly revived by the plant's closing bell, quickened in pace, rushing home full of verve to devote themselves to their classic car, garden, sports friends, or fellow musicians. Both models, but especially model 2, will represent this new world of work, in which qualified people, assigned to exciting tasks and acting on their own responsibility, can work with pleasure and in the interests of their companies.

2.5 Software, Algorithms, and Artificial Intelligence

Software and algorithms originally go back to developments made in the 1930s to 1950s (cf. Fig. 2.3). The term "artificial intelligence" was already coined back then. To this day, it has not been precisely defined nor delimited from a scientific point of view, and various approaches exist that focus on different aspects of Artificial Intelligence (AI). Accordingly, there are just as many different, mostly unclear, conceptions of this term in existence today.

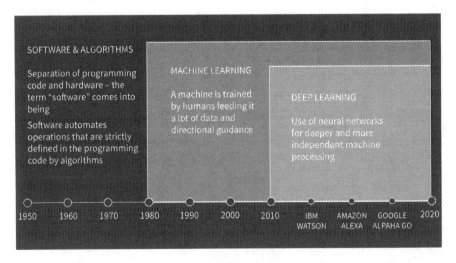

Fig. 2.3 Evolution of software, algorithms, and artificial intelligence

2.5 Software, Algorithms, and Artificial Intelligence

A classic definition comes from Alan Turing (1950), a pioneer in computer science who developed a fundamental, groundbreaking model of a computer in 1950. He wrote that artificial intelligence exists when one can no longer distinguish whether one is interacting with a human being or a machine.

Here we can see that it naturally depends on the application, the programmer, and the recipient to what extent it is possible to detect that something is the product of artificial intelligence or not. For instance, an example from the 1960s shows that a computer program that simply repeated questions or asked basic ones was perceived by some individuals to be a real human being. Real emotions were triggered, for example, with questions such as, "Why did your wife leave you?" (Weizenbaum, 1966).

Thus, this was not yet a case of a classically intelligent algorithm. For that is exactly the point where "real" artificial intelligence begins. Initially, it is about feeding data into a system to get meaningful decisions. Based on the consequences of those decisions, the system learns what was a right decision and what was a wrong one, which leads it to make ever better decisions. If there is enough data for performing a large number of learning sequences, the computer can learn very quickly and thus continuously improve its results.

Initially, it is up to humans to feed the data to the AI system, that is, to choose which data is useful and which is not. Since we live in a world of ever-increasing volumes of data, artificial intelligence—like humans—is constantly faced with the problem of information overflow: which information do I need to solve a problem— and which not? Everyone is familiar with this today, especially when dealing with the constant flood of emails, some of which contain important and highly relevant information, whereas others are completely worthless, especially those addressed as "an email to all." In the following sections, we will look more closely at how algorithms, statistical methods, and neural networks work as a basis for revealing the subsequent developmental stages of artificial intelligence.

2.5.1 What Is an Algorithm?

A simple way to understand an algorithm is to think of it as a recipe. For example, there are many ways to bake a cake. However, if we follow a recipe, we must first preheat the oven, choose the type of flour, weigh up the right amount of it as well as the right amount of butter, raisins, etc., and then bake the cake for a set amount of time at a set temperature until it is done.

A programmer or computer scientist can use algorithms, for example, to instruct his or her computer to query a database for last month's sales figures, compare them with the previous month and the same month last year, and then display them in a bar graph. So when several algorithms are combined, we get a working program that solves for us a practical task that is usually of a rather monotonous nature and where we often make mistakes due to distraction or fatigue.

The many types of algorithms are as diverse as these tasks. Algorithms can be developed for virtually any type of task that can be solved mathematically. There are numerical, geometric, algebraic, and sequential algorithms, bidirectional search algorithms, so-called operational algorithms, and many more. Theoretically, there is no limit. Many groundbreaking algorithms have been named after the leading mathematicians who invented them (Euclid, Shor, Girvan-Newman).

Most algorithms used in businesses today solve data management and analysis problems based on the following processes:

- Create, edit, display, and delete data
- Search data
- Sort and analyze data
- Convert larger, complex tasks into a series of smaller tasks
- Identify patterns and clusters in large data sets

Thus, all software is also based on an algorithm. It interacts either with humans, time, or some other connected system. For example, the software carries out a task every day at 10:00 a.m., or a human gives commands via a mouse using a graphical user interface, or another system triggers the software. That's all we need to know about software in this context. It is always the algorithm that then uses the data to do the job and generates further data, which is then stored in some kind of data repository.

The basic principle of "classical" software algorithms is based on a very large number of *if/then* decisions. Intelligent software algorithms learn based on an operating environment and a database, changing their decisions based on the available data. Using the spam filter as an example, if the word "Viagra" is in the email, it is 99% spam. If I have a pharmaceutical company, the word "Viagra" will not indicate spam to me. Likewise, if I have erectile dysfunction. An intelligent algorithm must make this learning process possible.

2.5.2 Artificial Intelligence for Decision Makers

Recently, more and more algorithms capable of learning have been used (in the sense of artificial intelligence) that enable changes to be made in the ongoing operation of systems, e.g., in response to certain workload situations—as explained using the example of intelligent spam filters. Thus, algorithms are already at the heart of almost everything that happens in the increasingly digitized world. From Google to Facebook and Amazon to intelligent control systems for building technology: for instance, to detect an approaching storm and retract awnings in time, close tilted windows, and lower aluminum exterior shutters for safety against hail.

These technologies are becoming increasingly ubiquitous. We rely more and more in our daily lives on smartphones, kitchen appliances, lawnmowers, cars, homes, cities, and increasingly even body implants. They're all just numbers and calculations—but we're already starting to communicate and feel with these systems: We get annoyed when they don't do exactly what we want them to do, and we are pleased when they dutifully do everything quickly. For example, Siri sometimes understands me wonderfully and immediately sends me the phone

2.5 Software, Algorithms, and Artificial Intelligence

	Web 1	Web 2	Web 3
sell	1		
affordable	1		
Bicycles	1	1	
repair		1	
old		1	
offer			1
E-Bike			1
Tours			1
search			

Indexing web pages and texts

Web 1: Sell affordable bicycles
Web 2: Repair old bicycles
Web 3: Offer e-bike tours

Fig. 2.4 Analysis of texts or web pages

number of the next delivery pizza service. Sometimes, however, she can't even solve the simplest problem, like telling me where my car key is. Then the algorithm surprises us again: When a 6-year-old says to her, "You're boring!" Siri replies, "I'm juggling fireballs right now, you just can't see it!"

With its uncompromising use of artificial intelligence, data giant Google has impressively and highly successfully shown the world that this technology is market-ready and can improve all of our lives. In the early days of the Internet, starting in the mid-1990s, data volumes increased tremendously. It became increasingly difficult to find one's way through the jungle of websites and get to the destination desired. Larry Page and Sergey Brin, both computer science students, provided a mathematical solution. In an environment of already existing competitors such as Yahoo, AlltheWeb, and Lycos, they programmed an adaptive search engine based on the "vector space model," which delivered by far the best results in the shortest time due to its complex capture and interpretation of content.

The system constructs a matrix that covers all the words in a language worldwide. Then all web pages are analyzed and the words they contain are entered into this matrix. Take our example for Web page 1: "Sell affordable bicycles" (see Fig. 2.4). A number series is generated from this short text which is mathematically interpreted as a vector and which "looks" into the huge language space, consisting of billions of

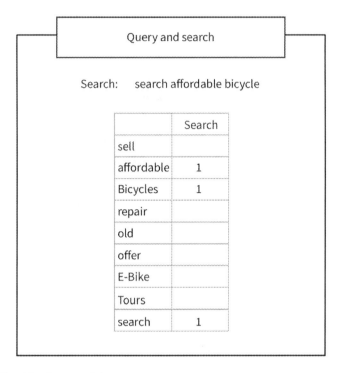

Fig. 2.5 Searching for a search term

word lists. My search term "search affordable bicycle" thus also results in a vector. I can now compare this vector with all the web page vectors already captured by capturing the angles between the vectors. The greater the similarity of two texts, the more likely the vectors point in a similar direction and the smaller the angle between the vectors (cf. Fig. 2.5).

The smaller the angle between the vectors, the better the search result. Google therefore calculates those hits that have the smallest possible angle to one another (cf. Fig. 2.6). In this way, all websites in the world were and continue to be stored in a matrix, and the Google robot "indexes" the website and files it away. Of course, Google's algorithm is only roughly similar to the very simplified algorithm described above. With strong statistical and mathematical algorithms, calculation time and search result have been significantly improved in the past decades. The system is constantly learning from ever more parameters how it can improve, for instance, how long people actually stay on the hit page—or whether they immediately move on. With this Google algorithm, the founding duo succeeded in best capturing human information needs and learnt to distinguish good websites from bad ones. To this day, the algorithm continues to evolve—and is likely also used regularly by the readers of this book.

A short anecdote illustrating the basic principle of artificial intelligence vividly and quite simply comes from the author's own history. Back then, I had programmed

2.5 Software, Algorithms, and Artificial Intelligence

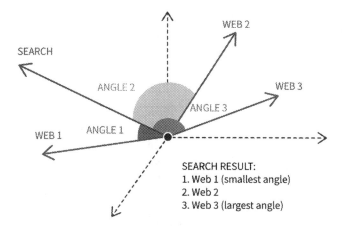

Fig. 2.6 Vector space model of all documents and the search query

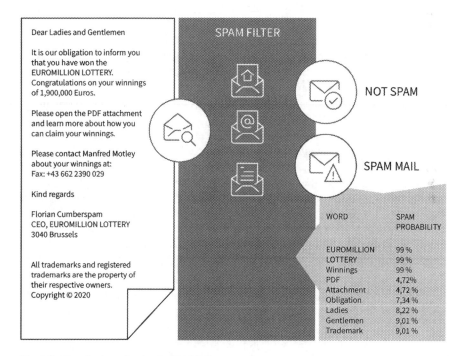

Fig. 2.7 Functioning of a simple SPAM filter

a self-learning spam filter (cf. Fig. 2.7). Now what does this program do? The program analyzes the individual words in an email and stores them along with the email. The system then receives human input: A person brings in his or her experience and tells the program that specific emails represent spam. Accordingly, for each word in this email, the algorithm remembers from now on that it has already occurred once in a spam email. The more often the users now give feedback to the system, the more the system can store probability values for individual words.

When a new email is analyzed, all of its words are analyzed along with their probability values. For example, if the word "Euromillions" appears, there is a 99% probability that it is spam. Based on the total result of all the words in an email, the system can independently decide whether it is a spam email or not.

This creates a two-way process: the system continues to learn autonomously based on user feedback, assigning a spam probability value to each word and then to the entire email. This is called "pattern recognition." Now I can define a threshold value above which emails end up in the digital trash folder. Further functionalities can be added to this simple and basic principle, based, for example, on the interrelationships of words (writing style), long and bulky sender addresses, or qualitative aspects of attachments (e.g., images).

However, one aspect remains very human even in this simple system: if the person who teaches the algorithm is sexist or racist, the judgment of the algorithm will also be sexist or racist. This can be well illustrated by another simple example: there are algorithms for selecting applications, for instance, which are basically structured in the same way as the spam filter. The system receives feedback from the fact of whether or not a person is actually hired, and the algorithm in turn learns from this. Now, if a racist hires only white employees, the algorithm also becomes racist by filtering out black applicants from the get-go.

In addition, algorithm-based decisions are easier to predict. This creates considerable strategic potential for companies. Today, for example, political parties also work with cluster algorithms to identify—on the basis of a large volume of data—certain types of voters with specific preferences. With the help of Cambridge Analytica, Donald Trump was able to reach those voters who might vote for him by sending them, via social media, personalized information relevant to the election. He already had secured the votes of other voters, and he wouldn't have stood a chance with sworn Democrats anyway (Wergin, 2018).

- The important message: as more and more decisions are made by algorithms, we need to understand the algorithms in order to understand the decisions.

Again, a simple example: a traffic light also works with algorithms based on the magnitude of traffic flows. If, as a road user, I know that I now have to wait three minutes because I have understood the algorithm, I will relax and use the time wisely. So if you understand the basic principle of algorithms, you will do well in today's world and especially in the future world and be able to generate significant advantages for yourself. Those who do not understand this will believe in magic, cosmic rays, or secret powers and will constantly feel cheated by the world.

The algorithms can also be the basis for developing products or putting together personalized offers, something that Amazon does at a very high level of sophistication. Amazon knows its customers like no other company. In contrast to traditional companies, customers are not clustered into hundreds of types, but are addressed and analyzed as individuals on the basis of their personal usage behavior and

2.5 Software, Algorithms, and Artificial Intelligence

preferences. This means that these individuals receive only those topic and product recommendations that precisely match their interests. This process is highly automated and based on a foundation that is continuously improved on the strength of ongoing experience (Is he or she really buying this now?). The product assortment is also continuously optimized on the basis of this experiential data. So it is not so much personal leadership qualities that have made Jeff Bezos the richest man in the world, but rather his skill in harnessing the many different capabilities of artificial intelligence.

2.5.3 Neural Networks and Deep Learning

So far, we have talked a lot about mathematics and statistics, about cluster algorithms and the like. Now we go one step further, and onto neural networks. These are basically "thick as a brick." They consist of nothing other than interconnected nodes, with the network making decisions based on these connections (cf. Fig. 2.8). But how do these decisions come about? Each node is tasked with continuously taking "inventory," a process that works on the basis of a very simple mathematical construct (Gasteiger & Zupan, 1999).

The term "deep learning" refers to a neural network, to the linking together of multiple layers and algorithms to reach a higher level of intelligence beyond simple tasks (see Fig. 2.9). Let's take image recognition as an example: a digital image has a bitmap (file extension ".bmp"). This bitmap consists of dots of more or less high resolution that have different colors and gray values. If you now take this bitmap and feed it to an inventory node, the latter looks at the individual points and recognizes, for example, whether a point is light or dark. It passes this information on to its neighboring node. This node again takes inventory and determines whether there is a contrast here or not, allowing it, in further steps at several points, to determine

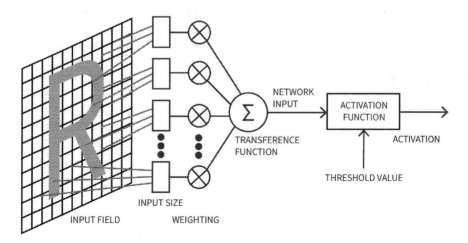

Fig. 2.8 A simple node in the neural network

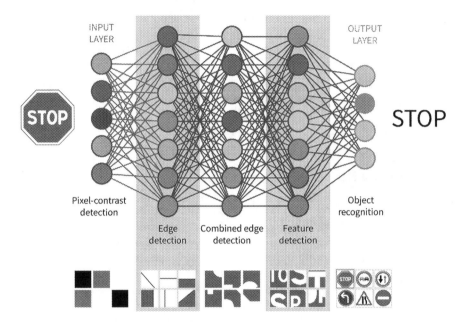

Fig. 2.9 How a deep learning neural network works

whether the picture exhibits a line. In even further steps it can be detected how sharply or subtly the line distinguishes itself from its surroundings, and whether it is straight or bent. Then it can be detected whether it might be a nose or an ear, how many noses or ears there are, and whether it might be a face. By being exposed to many facial images, the system learns to recognize which features a bitmap (or part of a bitmap) must have to represent a face. Finally—by using a database—these faces can also be assigned to specific persons, something that already works very well in photo programs and is already being used on a large scale in public spaces in China.

In principle, this learning process was invented decades ago, but today it is still state of the art and the basis for a wide variety of artificial intelligence applications. For example, the self-driving car works on the basis of this image recognition, whereby the volume of images with which the system learns is constantly increasing, thus continually reducing its error rate. As recently as 2017, the first self-driving Tesla processed 70,000 images in learning the algorithm; today it processes several million. In the future—and to some extent already—the self-learning traffic light will also analyze the latest data from satellite images on traffic flows and adapt its traffic light intervals to the prevailing road situation.

2.5.4 Application Areas for Artificial Intelligence

By means of learning algorithms and artificial intelligence, the company is continuously being taken to the next evolutionary level. This affects strategic areas of the company, the business model, interaction with the customer, and value-creating processes and production. Thanks to artificial intelligence, it is possible to take continuous improvement processes to a new level: processes, results, and work models optimize themselves by means of new algorithms during ongoing operations.

Based on many years of consulting experience with large corporations, public organizations, and mid-sized companies, best practices and clusters for the use and deployment of artificial intelligence algorithms have emerged (see Fig. 2.10). In addition to the typical classifications of learning algorithms into strong and weak (or general and narrow) artificial intelligence, the literature often categorizes them according to methods or learning behavior. Among AI methods, one can distinguish symbolic AI, the phenomenological method, neural AI, and the simulation method. All these categorizations refer to the technical implementation of the cognitive algorithm. Our experience has shown that it makes more sense for companies to cluster algorithms by application area. The *RAPD* framework has emerged from this line of thinking. Here, artificial intelligence algorithms are classified into the following four domains and thus fulfill similar applications:

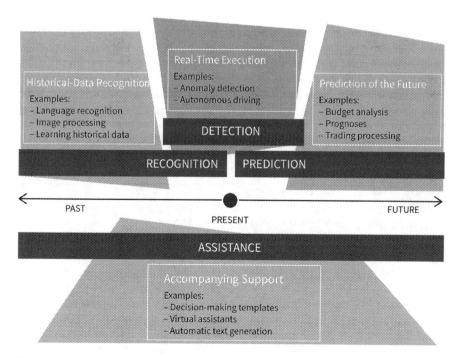

Fig. 2.10 Categorization of learning algorithms according to RAPD

- Recognition (R)
- Assistance (A)
- Prediction (P)
- Detection (D)

In cases of recognition, cognitive algorithms are used to detect historical events. Typical examples are the detection of data theft based on log files or the enrichment of images with additional information. The algorithms are applied to historical data sets.

Assistance refers to accompanying support. Data from the past, the present, and from extrapolated forecast data are included in the decision. Typical cases of application involve virtual assistants and algorithms that make decision recommendations.

Prediction algorithms are based on historical data, but use them to simulate and project future trends and events. Budget forecasts and planning are calculated with prediction algorithms. Trend analysis of stocks or electricity prices also fall into this category.

Detection algorithms analyze data in real time. These algorithms are also trained with historical data, but decide in real time when new real-time data is available. In industry, these software solutions have been in use for years, such as for the detection of product anomalies on a conveyor belt. Autonomous driving represents another example.

2.5.5 Requirements for Intelligent Algorithms

The most important requirements for intelligent algorithms are the comprehensibility and predictability of decisions. Only if these properties are achieved will society accept these software systems. Decisions that are not comprehensible will not be accepted by users or by those affected. For this reason, apart from any technical requirements, these cognitive algorithms must also meet certain emotional and sociopolitical requirements. These range from the explicit inclusion of software programming in all school curricula to the education of society as a whole about how it works. Only an enlightened and knowledgeable society will be able to interact successfully with this future technology.

As can be seen from the previous sections, these algorithms and deep learning processes require considerable computer power. However, it can be assumed that computer capacities will continue to increase rapidly in the future. For the development of computing power follows exponential curves. An new iPhone in use today has the capacity that would have required an entire data center just a few years ago. If we go back even further in time, we soon arrive at gigantic computing units that provided only one millionth of the power of an iPhone. They still had mechanical switches that opened and closed with a clatter, and the units filled entire halls. This is where the term "software bug" comes from. If a beetle sat on a switch, the latter could not make contact resulting in an error in the program. Employees then had to search for these squashed bugs and remove them by hand. A nice example of how

2.5 Software, Algorithms, and Artificial Intelligence

job profiles change as technology evolves. More on this in connection with the vision of the self-driving company in Sect. 6.5.

When I originally wrote this book in German in 2020, computing power roughly equaled that of the mouse brain. Since the outbreak of the Corona pandemic in the spring of 2020, we have become well acquainted with exponential rates of growth. Computing power is also growing at a similar exponential rate, and we can expect the so-called "singularity" to occur in 2024–2026. This means that the computer will be more powerful than the human brain. By 2050, computing power will be equal to that of all human brains taken together. From that point on, the number of highly automated—though not yet self-driving—companies will grow by leaps and bounds (Kraikivski, 2019).

How well artificial intelligence already works in everyday applications can be seen in speech recognition, which any cell phone or word processor can now provide. We should first note that the translation of spoken language into written language is an extraordinarily complex problem. It requires the system to correctly decode phonetic signals, and this alone represents a considerable challenge. For hardly any language is phonetically precise, and many words are written completely differently than they are pronounced, especially in English. Moreover, there are so-called homophones, words that sound exactly the same but are spelled differently: two, to, too, or air and heir. Furthermore, English possesses a wide range of distinct pronunciations from British to U.S. American English, from Canadian to Australian English, to the English of the Celtic fringe, just to mention a few. And this does not begin to cover the amazing diversity in pronunciation, vocabulary, and syntax created by English as the global lingua franca. Thus, to decode a sentence correctly, the system must actively think along. Your average student in the U.S. has built up an active vocabulary of roughly 10,000 words by the time he or she graduates from high school, which represents 17 or 18 years of conversational practice. However, this does not mean that they can take down dictation without making mistakes. In the meantime, speech recognition systems have reached a level that is on a par with the average person—and will soon far outstrip him or her. This process of actively thinking along about the meaning of a statement requires a tremendous amount of computing power. The iPhone, for example, sends the phonetic data to Apple's data center, where it is analyzed, interpreted, and sent back to the smartphone in the form of text. If you are not yet familiar with this function, you should try it out right now. This book was also largely created using this voice input system. This eliminates the need now and in the future for humans to carry out the encoding process, for example, by transforming their thoughts into letters. They can reproduce these thoughts in the form of the language they consider more developmentally favorable for themselves and the system relieves them of the encoding work. There are other advantages, too: in the future, we will have our hands free when writing, will be able to read a text and simultaneously reproduce it in our own words, and will no longer have to worry too much about spelling. Google and Co. now take care of that. As our own experience shows, it's enough to simply read what the system writes and correct words that were misunderstood by speech recognition. As I write, this is a maximum of two to three words per page and tending downwards. Punctuation marks such as "period" and "comma" still need to be announced as such, although this will no longer be necessary in the foreseeable future.

Artificial intelligence will still be based at its core on algorithms, but—due to the enormous computing power required—will ultimately result from the networking of subsystems, as we see in the speech recognition (voice input) system. The Corona pandemic of 2020, for example, demonstrated how millions of cell phones can be networked together to identify interactions that are relevant according to specific criteria. As the number of network points increases, the required computing power increases exponentially.

The challenge for companies will be to identify and implement these opportunities. With Industry 4.0, the first steps in this direction have already been taken over the past two decades. Whereas production used to be managed largely manually through expertise and experience, the technological enhancements of Industry 4.0 now enable management to interact in real time and respond immediately to changes and individual requirements.

2.6 What Comes After Industry 4.0 and Digitization?

The self-driving company is the long-term evolution of the two trends of Industry 4.0 and digitization. In this respect, it continues to follow the "classic" principles of industrialization:

- Automation
- Standardization
- Modularization
- Specialization
- Continuous optimization

In order to understand this developmental step, it is first necessary to explain in more detail what Industry 4.0 is all about, especially because very different ideas about it can be found circulating in companies. Many entrepreneurs are confused by this term and torn between sticking to the tried and true and actively exploring these opportunities.

The scientific definition of Industry 4.0 is also broad: it is referred to as another industrial revolution or as the fourth industrial revolution of our time. Put simply, it is a process based on the digitization of industrial operations. This is achieved through the use of sensors, intelligent algorithms, and the analysis of large data sets in conjunction with machine-based production. Another aspect of Industry 4.0 is the optimization of resources with the help of economic strategies based on ongoing data analysis. Based on recent evaluations, it has been shown that the introduction of these digital technologies can reduce costs in production plants by between 15% and 20% (Obermaier, 2019).

One of the main goals of Industry 4.0 and a key advantage is the constant, rapid adaptability of the entire value chain to changing customer demand. If, for example,

2.6 What Comes After Industry 4.0 and Digitization?

a BMW is sold in Vienna, this information is immediately sent in automated form to all global suppliers, who in turn adapt their production lines, resources, and subcontractors to the new situation. In this way, the production and sale of products or services take place in a significantly shorter time, while at the same time quality improves.

The vision of Industry 4.0 is the production of a batch size of one—in other words, customization in series production. Through software-supported manufacturing processes, this kind of individualized production can now be achieved at the cost of series production. This results in the following aspects of Industry 4.0, aspects that provide companies with significant advantages:

- Design: Consumer demands are increasingly individualized and also influenced by cultural aspects. For example, a BMW for the Chinese market must meet requirements that already go far beyond those in Europe, especially in the area of electromobility and self-driving. With Industry 4.0, product design is directly networked with sales and all other relevant production functions.
- More personal customer service: in general, customer service employees will be relieved of the burden of dealing with technology, allowing them to engage customers in a more personal relationship.
- Implementation of additional services for physical products (product service systems, PSS 4.0): it has long been possible, for example, to visualize—in advance and true to the original—the model with all elements of special equipment and to obtain in advance a digital twin.
- The possibility of continuously analyzing the customer relationship: The results can be measured in a host of ways, including via CMS (Content Management Systems), SCM (Supply Chain Management), CRM (Customer Relationship Management), FCM (Financial Capital Management) and social media.
- The Internet of Things, for instance, can be used—with the help of sensors—to collect information on the various elements of the production chain, which can subsequently optimize the production process.
- The coordination of logistics and production tasks is being automated and optimized in more and more areas through the introduction of robots and full mechatronic automation.
- By means of Big Data analyses—based on data from far beyond the confines of the company—processes can be further optimized, energy consumption improved, and production quality in the factories increased.
- Conversely, thanks to cloud-based platform software systems, data can be stored beyond the confines of the company and shared with other subsidiaries around the world, allowing, for example, product teams to work together on improvements across national borders.
- While these "hyperconnections" have opened up great opportunities, at the same time, critical areas must be protected from cyber threats. Therefore, it is important to integrate secure communications with highly secure identity and access management systems.

- Additive manufacturing—3D printing—for example, ensures that all kinds of parts made from different materials can be produced in hollow structures that would otherwise be impossible to manufacture in one piece. Moreover, they can be produced directly based on design. This makes it possible to create completely new products, including 3D-printed houses, such as the one already completed in Dubai in February 2020. In addition, such opportunities will decentralize small-scale production processes. The blueprint of a product can be "downloaded," "printed out" at the nearest post office, and delivered in a matter of minutes.

All of these opportunities that have emerged in conjunction with Industry 4.0 can, of course, also be implemented in the self-driving company. They represent, however, just a first step in the context of much further-reaching prospects. To demonstrate this with a small example: As indicated above, Industry 4.0 enables customer relationships to be measured and interpreted via social media responses. At present, this is only possible in very simple, numerical dimensions, for example, by recording the number of "likes." Up until now, more in-depth analyses of the content of comments, images, and dialogs have had to be carried out by the individual efforts of coworkers. By means of artificial intelligence, this is becoming more and more fully automated in the self-driving company and networked with all related systems. If, for example, a significant number of BMW drivers criticize the fact that unwanted noises crop up at a certain speed, these findings are immediately fed into the development process, where the effect is tested and improvements are introduced.

It is a fact that, in recent decades, medium-sized companies in Germany, Austria, and Switzerland have invested very heavily in issues relating to Industry 4.0 production and value creation processes. As a result, software-driven optimization potentials in other business areas have often been neglected, and there has been no or only weak use of strong potentials for optimizing companies. This book highlights these potentials and outlines best practices.

In the self-driving company a kind of total organism comes into being, possessing high perceptual abilities both inside and outside the company. In this way, the company, seen as a whole, basically becomes ever more similar to a human being. After all, our thinking and feeling is not fragmented into sub-areas, but takes place holistically. When we are confronted with the task of climbing a steep mountain, the immediate assessment is whether we are capable of doing it at all, whether we have the right equipment for it, and what amount of food is required. This occurs without having to send messages back and forth between the individual areas responsible for musculature, the oxygen-carrying capacity of the blood, heart volume, stomach contents, and risk management in the cerebral cortex, or to mountain sports and food suppliers.

2.7 Why Software-Driven Companies?

Software solves many of the current problems facing companies and makes work more livable again.

2.7 Why Software-Driven Companies?

This statement can be supported by a number of findings. First, software-driven companies follow proven market and social rules and are thus more likely to be resilient than human-driven companies. They make fewer mistakes and react less impulsively than humans do in many of their decisions. This circumstance has already been well researched in the field of behavioral economics. Humans are only capable of making the best economic decision to a limited degree. Especially in the presence of a large volume of information, or in cases of stress and/or anxiety—that is, in what has hitherto been everyday office life—considerable bias effects have become apparent:

- Information overload: In the presence of too much information, limited cognitive resources mean that only a small amount of information, and often the less relevant part, is used to make decisions that, as a result, are incorrect.
- Stereotyping: Humans tend to assign new information to known typologies. In doing so, they prefer stereotypes that are well known and familiar—even if the new information does not fit into the scheme at all. Our prejudices are also based on this principle. Since this process usually takes place unconsciously, it is particularly difficult to recognize these effects and to reflect on them objectively.
- Anchor effect: "First impressions are lasting"—if a person is confronted with a new situation, the first assessment has a lasting effect on further assessments, even if this first assessment turns out to be wrong.
- Halo effect: Individual aspects of a situation are often subjectively perceived by the person concerned as having a particularly strong effect ("casting a halo," as it were). The dominance of this impression subsequently distorts all further decisions in this context.
- Risky shift effect: This effect shows how individual decisions differ from group decisions, even if both are based on the same data. In team decisions, there is a strong tendency towards consensus and unanimity. Team members strive to avoid conflicts, while the focus is on arguments that promote harmony and mutually reinforce each other. This group behavior results in systematically ignoring possible risks and leads to wrong or risky decisions.
- Mental accounts: This effect can best be explained with an example. If you buy a concert ticket for 100 € and you lose it on the way to the opera, you will probably not buy a new one. If you don't have a ticket yet and lose 100 € on the way, in rational terms, you have exactly the same loss as in the case of the lost ticket. Nevertheless, in this case, you behave completely differently and buy a ticket for another 100 €. Why do we do this? The explanation is that we keep different mental accounts when making decisions. In the case study, these are two accounts, one for the "ticket" and one for the 100 € invested. If the admission ticket is lost, there will be a total loss of the 100 €, and the account is left overdrawn. However, if the 100 € are lost, the loss is related to the mental account "total assets" and is considered only marginally relevant. This simple example shows that even in a completely simple situation in economic terms, we decide irrationally due to our subconscious heuristics.

In addition to these effects, countless wrong decisions occur due to psychological tensions in hierarchically organized organizations, and due to conflicts and diverse human motives. The American psychologist Steven Reiss (2004) identified 16 motives that influence our everyday actions:

- Power: the pursuit of leadership, influence, success, achievement
- Independence: freedom, self-sufficiency
- Curiosity: knowledge, truth
- Recognition: social belonging, acceptance, positive self-esteem
- Order: stability, organization, clarity
- Saving: accumulation of material values, goods, property
- Honor: moral integrity, loyalty
- Idealism: fairness, social justice
- Relationships: joy, friendship, humor
- Family: family, education of children
- Status: wealth, prestige, titles, public attention
- Revenge: competition, aggression, struggle, retaliation
- Eros: erotic life, attractiveness, sexuality
- Food: Food, refined cooking
- Physical activity: fitness, movement
- Rest: relaxation, emotional security

Computers, on the other hand, have no prejudices and do not hold grudges. Software always listens, attentively, to everyone. It does not get tired, and even works through the night and on weekends. There are no human conflicts with management; computers always have all the necessary data and decide strictly rationally and mathematically, as far as we grant them this freedom. So software is the perfect micro-manager and yet can pursue global and strategic goals if we program it to do so. In addition, the software can also take countermeasures in the event of human error. Surveys and analyses of human behavior are used to identify weaknesses and dissatisfaction in the company at an early stage, and countermeasures can be taken quickly.

This also means serious changes for the personnel. Middle, operational, and tactical management will be replaced by algorithms and software. As a result, careers will become more "objectives-oriented" and flatter: they will be based on the ability to achieve the key, set objectives with the team in accordance with overarching goals. In addition, the activities of the team members will be enhanced in value. With the complete transparency created by the software, more emphasis will be placed on the direct benefits of any activity for the organization as a whole. This also means that the struggles for advancement by means of ingratiation and intrigue that are common in traditional organizations will be transformed into positive energy. As a result, owners, shareholders, and those entitled to bonuses also benefit from the higher productivity of self-driving companies.

2.7.1 Cost Effects and Marginal Effects

If the self-driving enterprise did not generate positive effects on costs, the vision would probably not be very attractive for companies. The effects are based on the ongoing improvement and also acceleration of all operational functions. Of course, this will mean that fewer people will be required in operational, manual roles (for more on this, see Sect. 2.7.2). Overall, in any case, there will also be significant cost effects in terms of personnel, since all routines will be automated and improvements will also be made in the efficiency of those people remaining in the organization.

For example, in the self-organized team (Sect. 6.5.1), team coordination is continuously optimized—and in the so-called software-guided team (Sect. 6.5.2) prefabricated and continuously improved operating instructions can be created automatically, considerably speeding up on-site repairs among other things.

The company's coworkers will earn considerably more than they did in 2000–2020, as the contribution margin has also risen due to the increased value added per coworker. Currently, this is already demonstrated by the pioneers of digital business, such as Apple: The company creates almost $two million in revenue per coworker per year. With its 137,000 employees, Apple generates $260 billion in revenue per year (Fortune, 2020).

A lot of the investment budget and work will initially be involved in programming and implementing these intelligent and networked software systems. Especially the programming of software systems is standardized worldwide and thus easily distributable. The programming languages Java or Phyton are spoken the same way all over the world and IT systems also interpret them identically—regardless of the origin of the program code. Accordingly, these services can just as well be provided by Indian programmers or African software developers instead of Austrians, Germans, or the even more expensive Swiss programmers. The human cost factor will be decisive in the choice of software origin. However, the analytic work and integration services will be provided by regional service providers. After the algorithms are implemented and integrated into the companies, the programming tasks will shift to the interaction between self-driving companies. Software investments have already become an important budget item for companies in recent years. The vision of the self-driving company proves the importance of software investments and assumes that software investments will rise to levels roughly comparable to those of investments in real estate and machinery. In the future, investments in software will also be calculated and depreciated over a longer period of time. My consulting experience with large corporations and enterprises shows that the recommended referencing period for business-critical software systems (e.g., ERP systems, CRM systems, backend systems) is around 15 years. A return on investment for these business-critical backend software systems cannot be expected in less than 5–10 years. This can only be expected, in such a short period of time, for websites, customer portals, simple apps, web stores, or software solutions for digital business models.

2.7.2 Effects on Different Roles

The new distribution of tasks initially has the effect of flattening hierarchies in companies, simply because many second-level management tasks are handled by algorithms. One structural feature that remains is the team. Within these self-organized teams, team members have the same position and work together as equals. Purchasing is self-organizing, as are maintenance and sales. Being freed up from routines allows people to increasingly use their core competencies of empathy and creativity, areas in which they will remain unrivaled by any kind of artificial intelligence in the near future. Many of the most successful companies are already relying on these flat hierarchies, on informal, empathic communication and the creativity this generates. Because ultimately, the decisions and directional inputs will always come from people, even in self-driving companies.

Another key difference to previous companies will be that the self-driving company will no longer have a single IT department. The central elements, the data and algorithms, will flow through the veins of the company like blood. No longer will software experts and techno nerds sit in the IT department and administer the systems. The software will just be applied in the individual departments—but at a higher level, deciding how a particular algorithm will be used in the overall system. There will no longer be any need for debit and credit postings; this will all be taken care of by networked algorithms in a self-governing manner.

Whereas in the past, for example, a new co-worker had to be added to the system in many individual steps by an IT specialist, in the future a one-step approval procedure will suffice to create a fully functional workstation. No more CDs that have to be manually inserted into the drive at some point, no more manual installation of programs downloaded from the Internet.

There will be no need for costly software training, as use will be highly intuitive, such as through an artificial intelligence-driven voice recognition system that will completely replace keyboard typing. It's an evolutionary step like that from manually typed DOS commands to a fully graphical screen. The people working for the self-driving company will only need to reach a basic understanding of what their IT is capable of—just like they have reached a basic understanding of how to use their seven senses, their knowledge, their minds, and their hands and feet to bake a cake. Here, too, everything works in sync without the stomach having to first send a hunger message to the brain, which it then approves, followed by a project team meeting of knowledge, mind, eyes, hands and feet at which it is discussed who has to solve which further tasks and when.

2.7.3 Subjectively Perceived Threats from Self-Driving Companies

As can be seen indirectly from the explanations, the profound changes also give rise to subjectively perceived threats:

- Many existing jobs need to be reconceived. Some jobs will be upgraded in terms of content since the tedious routines will be taken over by the software and one can concentrate on the exciting empathic and creative activities. Other jobs are increasingly defined and delegated by software systems. Here, the software algorithm will take over quality and performance control.
- About 20%–30% of current "positions" will be eliminated. Previous moments of technical evolution show us, however, that new fields of activity will likely be created to the same or possibly even greater extent.
- The words "(job) position" and "employee" will no longer exist in the twenty-first century in their current meaning. The flexibility of the world of work is increasing spatially, temporally, and in terms of content.
- People will be resistant against algorithms if they're seen to be "incomprehensible." Throughout human history, when something is not understood, it is always drawn into the "mystical." The highly comprehensible nature of the functionality of algorithms (as exemplified by voice input instead of keyboard) will increasingly ensure acceptance.
- Algorithms will also make unpleasant decisions in the company, such as giving notice to employees. They will be able to justify these layoffs transparently, fairly, and comprehensibly.

The decisions of algorithms will also raise legal issues, for instance, in the event of an accident with a self-driving car or an unplanned system outage. The "who's at fault?" question will have to be reconceived in legal terms. Legislative changes will provide solutions to this problem, and insurance companies will offer products to cover these unusual and infrequently occurring damage claims.

2.7.4 When Is a Company Considered Self-Driving?

Once a company has reached a level of about 80% software penetration, it can be said to be self-driving. That is, if 80% or more of the operational functions and decisions are automated and guided by sufficiently intelligent algorithms, the company is self-driving. Reality will reveal, however, that it is not as a whole that companies go through the various stages of evolution, but rather in their individual areas, departments, or teams. Thus, the various areas are likely to have different characteristics.

The following example of invoicing should illustrate the different prerequisites: If the invoice is traditionally sent by mail, then there is no digital basis on which to proceed. One would speak of an analog company. If the invoice arrives as a PDF by e-mail, then the company is already one step further. The algorithm can learn to recognize the invoices and assign them to the invoicing company. Then the digital company can check automatically whether this service was actually provided by the invoicing company to the same extent as requested and release the invoice for payment, which is also done by means of an algorithm. Human interaction may occasionally still be required in a self-driving company that is in the early stages of automation; for example, if the company issuing the invoice changes its logo, an error message will come up and the staff member responsible will check the invoice and release the new version. The algorithm is now familiar with the new version and will subsequently process all subsequent iterations of it correctly. This automation allows the process of invoice receipt to be completely resolved.

In the fully self-driving enterprise, the system of outgoing and incoming invoices between two companies will also be reconceived. Platforms will provide for the fully digital and automatic exchange of this information between the two ERP (enterprise resource planning) systems. The data will be available at all times with the contracts associated with them, and documents will no longer be generated. This process could be compared to the flow of money. Here, too, no physical units of money, no cash is exchanged, but only the data in software systems is rewritten. The invoicing process between companies will be similar. Artificial intelligence will check data such as partner ID, amounts to be paid, and purpose of the invoice against historical company data, budgeted values, and current procurements, requirements, and contracts.

Parts of operational functions will always remain in human hands, such as in-person consulting, which will always be face-to-face. Or complicated, individual construction, repair, and maintenance work at the customer's site. People will always be needed somewhere—for individual, interpersonal, motivating, and challenging activities, and those of high responsibility. But no longer for boring routines, because such routines allow at best for mistakes, but no real sense of achievement and no human growth, no development of real potential.

What is certain is that boundaries will be ever shifting. For example, even as a computer scientist, I have now turned largely into a car engineer: it is less and less the mechanic in the workshop with their wrench who tunes the car—but the computer scientist who gets more performance out of the engine with their software. This example shows how software is penetrating ever more deeply into environments we previously knew well, and how it will shape our future lives.

2.7.5 The Seven Central Propositions

In summary, we can draw the following central propositions from our findings so far:

1. People will continue to work in and for companies. They will perform the empathic and creative tasks.
2. Intelligent software algorithms are better suited to repetitive corporate tasks than humans.
3. There will be no more processes—processes are from the nineteenth and twentieth century: algorithms are the twenty-first century.
4. Middle management will be replaced by software—people will hold on to leadership tasks.
5. Software and IT are the basis for the self-driving enterprise. Therefore, central IT departments will be dissolved in their current form and IT tasks, software

development, and IT operations will become the responsibility of the company's specialized departments.
6. Missing jobs will be compensated for by demographic development and the growth of markets due to productivity gains.
7. Companies will still serve people in 2035.

2.8 Guidelines for Evolution

Today, companies in the classic sense can still be understood as partially digitized, which can be justified on the basis of their history. Even though many individual subdivisions are already completely paperless and thus digitized, even though they send e-mails and have an ERP system, the mode of operation itself is still based on the analog principles of collaboration. For example, file folders are scanned and digitized and no longer have to be stowed away in cabinets in paper form. Nevertheless, these files have not been formatted such that they can be used automatically, since software algorithms are not able to read and understand this data.

Definitionally, "digital" means that the data and information are prepared in a digital manner and are machine-readable and available for further processing, for example by an ERP or CRM system. Thus, although the scanned folder is now digital, it cannot be read and processed by a machine. In this case, to understand the content or semantics, a crutch is needed, such as image or text recognition.

Accordingly, most companies today find themselves in an early position between the analog and digital worlds (cf. Fig. 2.11). Companies follow the "trend of digitization" in their thinking only in so far as converting data that previously existed in paper form into digital data. However, this state of affairs is still miles away from the self-driving company:

1. First, a "true" digital enterprise must be created, with all data in machine-readable and processable form. On this basis, the machine can then understand syntax and

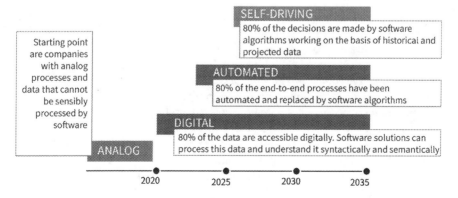

Fig. 2.11 Definition of the evolutionary stages to autonomy

semantics. A digital enterprise can be said to exist when about 80% of all data is in this digital form. This also means that many companies today have not yet reached this stage themselves. The scanned invoice, as progressive as it is, is just an image that cannot be further processed digitally. This is the challenge that most companies are currently facing.

2. The next step is automation, in which processes or problems are handled by programs. This first takes place via small partially automated processes, extending all the way to full automation, in which approximately 80% of all processes in the company are automated, for instance, by creating and transmitting outgoing invoices in data form without human intervention and checking that they are paid correctly. The remaining 20% consist of special cases that are still handled manually. Overall, important decisions outside of the scope of routines are still made or programmed by humans.

3. The final step toward the self-driving company is based on the fact that the data is not only available in readable form and processed by programs, but that algorithms make the decisions on the basis of historical data and these decisions are then adapted as a result of learning processes. This means that operational and tactical decisions are now made by the system as it learns—and this covers a considerably larger proportion of those special cases that previously could not be handled by the programs.

The term "self-driving" was therefore chosen deliberately. Although it is oriented toward the stages leading to the self-driving automobile, its objective is not quite as radical. In the case of vehicles, the highest of achievable levels would be the car that drives on its own. This approach should also be applied to companies at this point. Nevertheless, we are talking about developments that will not become achievable before 2035. The societal conditions and the estimated further developments needed for this idea are not foreseeable at this point in time. For this reason, we deliberately speak in this book of the vision of the self-driving company and thus remain at the level of what is reasonably feasible. People will continue to decide where the journey should head until 2035—the company will cope with these decisions in a self-driving way.

In the context of an enterprise or organization, self-driving means that the majority of decisions will be made on the basis of data from software with the help of algorithms and learning processes. In this context, the volume of data will be enormous due to the automated, ongoing collection of all internal system information throughout the company, and from all relevant stakeholders, and the use of Big Data. This will open up unimagined possibilities because the algorithms work extremely quickly and precisely—much more precisely than humans are able to do even with the much smaller data sets that currently still exist.

This is best illustrated with examples: We could not possibly control a drone in the form of a quadro- or multicopter by hand; too much data from too many sensors must be processed here simultaneously in order to continuously stabilize the aircraft and steer it unerringly (see Fig. 2.12).

2.8 Guidelines for Evolution

Fig. 2.12 Photo of a quadcopter drone (Kendall, 2020)

Even the self-driving car can already simultaneously collect and process significantly larger amounts of information than a human being could. Work is already underway on the remaining problems of interpreting special situations correctly, whereas the traffic rules that people cram for their driver's license test are learned by the system in a matter of seconds. They have exact knowledge of all maps, which are processed as road maps but also, thanks to Google, as satellite images and road views, with all the signs then correctly recorded and compared with the on-board camera even in the event of a snowstorm. In addition, light sensors continuously measure all distances around the vehicle, for example to walkers and cyclists. Today, entire cities already have self-driving public transport, such as Shenzhen in China, the Chinese "Silicon Valley," even if human "overseers" are usually still along for the ride. The individual vehicles learn continuously while in operation and share their experiences with all the other vehicles, learning, for example, how to deal with a piece of cloth that the wind blows across the roadway.

Experience shows that these systems are far safer than human drivers because they do not get tired, do not drink alcohol, and are not distracted by operating the GPS, eating, drinking, or making cell phone calls. Moreover, they make decisions strictly rationally and never out of anger or overconfidence. In the long run, then, traffic will become self-driving, and cars driven by humans will only be allowed on private racetracks.

So we are in the middle of a process and on the verge of handing over driving to a self-driving car. Only at the company level do we still believe that it's better to do everything by hand. Even though the only logical consequence of development is that everything that can be self-driving will sooner or later also be self-driving. Piloted by highly intelligent, highly adaptive, and reliable systems that are used exactly in those areas where they are far superior to humans.

If we perceive the process of digitization, moving steadily toward the digital enterprise, as rapid today, it is only because of our very limited planning horizon, which culminates with the transformation from analog to digital data. But this is

Fig. 2.13 Illustration of an exponential function

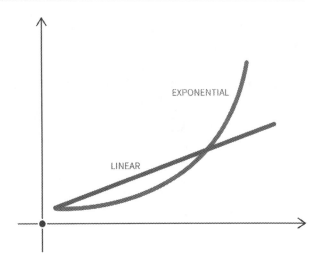

actually only the first step on the considerably longer path toward the self-driving company. If the planning horizon is extended to the self-driving company in 2035, we will notice that not very much is currently happening along these lines. However, an indispensable foundation is being laid that will result in exponential development (see Fig. 2.13). And this is precisely where the greatest challenge lies in the scenario described. "Mankind's greatest weakness is its inability to understand the exponential function," said physicist Al Bartlett in "The Essential Exponential!" (Bartlett, 2006).

This exponentiality sets in as more and more parts of the system take on a life of their own, learning, communicating with each other, and capturing and processing ever-increasing amounts of data in real time to meet business objectives. This means that little progress will be visible for a long time, but suddenly things will start to move incredibly quickly and steeply upwards. Ever more powerful computers will also make a significant contribution to this. Entrepreneurs, owners, decision-makers, and politicians must therefore learn today not just to think linearly in a 5-year horizon, but exponentially with a big vision in mind. Thus, self-driving companies will not only soon overtake analog, semi-digitized companies by moving at a consistently high speed, but will actually accelerate further in the process.

It will probably take until around 2030 for these changes to become visible, at which point the curve will start to rise steeply. Those companies that have not created a suitable basis by then will no longer be able to catch up. If they then only want to replace the old ERP system, they will have to reckon with a period of 4–5 years. The larger the companies are, the sooner they will have to start preparing for these major changes. Smaller companies will have an easier time of it in that they will purchase smaller-scale and cloud-based software products from the market that will feature these intelligent solutions and also provide the appropriate integration with other tools.

2.8 Guidelines for Evolution

Most companies will continue to be analog; the self-driving company is not a sensible vision for all business models. The small, exquisite workshop in an Alpine village will continue to make tailored buckskin *Lederhosen* by hand and then issue the invoice manually too. In doing so, however, the owner makes a conscious decision against global scalability and comes to terms with a limited growth potential. Presumably, he or she will find this work to be fulfilling. If the market now accepts these products at an exceptionally high price, the owner will also be able to make a comfortable living from them.

The big companies will have to go along with the change, otherwise they will disappear completely from the market, as, for instance, Nokia or Kodak did. Today's basic conditions will no longer allow them to cope in 2035: they will no longer be compatible with the digital interfaces to partner companies and government agencies, they will not be able to keep up with the extreme adaptability of their competitors, and they will no longer be able to meet the needs of their customers, who will now have become accustomed to having all their wishes professionally registered and understood by their providers. So today, the most important thing for companies to realize is that they need to get moving in their entirety. It is not enough to set up small digital units as lighthouse projects in an effort to keep the remaining stagnant parts of the company in the shadows. Instead, a complete restructuring of the company is required—not of the business model, but of the entire company. If the business model works today, it can initially be assumed that it will also work with the self-driving company.

The process must be radically implemented. Just digitizing 80% of all data in the company into a machine-readable and processable form represents a huge challenge. This challenge is all the greater when you consider that many companies have been digitizing since the mid-1990s, which means for more than 25 years now.

In general, one should not wait until a certain state of technology has been reached throughout the company. It is best to take action at different points or in different areas. If, for example, a digital CRM system has already been set up in sales, a start can be made on automating it, as in the case of automated contacting: Replies or newsletters can mark the beginning of the development. This does not necessarily mean, for example, that the text of the newsletter is generated automatically. Here it will still make sense to have it written by an expert.

Especially important and successful sales contacts will continue to take place from person to person. However, everything surrounding this, all those time-consuming routines, should be automated. For example, since 2015 it has already been technically possible to schedule appointments automatically: here time management software records the free appointment times of all parties involved and checks them for consistency, avoiding the often endless and repeated phone calls required when several people are involved. For the software, this is a snap, provided that all parties involved have the appropriate technical equipment. At the moment, however, there are only a few "early adopters" using this software—but it's only a matter of time before this becomes the new normal. This usually takes place when a certain benefit is available and a critical mass has been reached. A viral effect then occurs with such applications: just as before with Skype, Zoom, or WhatsApp, some users already possess this technology and ask their friends and business partners to also use this app so that they can communicate or cooperate better with each other. The better the app, the more quickly are these people convinced, and they, in turn, contact their friends and associates. The result is a snowball effect that quickly covers the entire globe.

The example of automated appointment setting shows an application in the field of automation. However, it is not yet an intelligent application. The appointment scheduling app would be intelligent if it learned from internal and external company data that certain people should make an appointment. If, for example, due to a large order received, the system determines that there are too few steel components in stock and that the existing supplier does not have additional capacity, this info, along with a proposed appointment with the other suppliers, is transmitted to the procurement agent, who gives the go-ahead with one click. Prior to this, the self-learning agent system had figured out, with a few seconds of worldwide research, who the best suppliers for these components were.

Similar functions are conceivable for all decisions that cannot be made directly by intelligent systems. Humans are called in, and they are informed about the situation, the need for action, and provided with concrete suggestions. In this way, for example, a software-guided maintenance technician would receive instructions, via their data glasses, on how and where to act if the maintenance cannot be carried out by the system itself.

Some people will be frightened by such a prospect. But if we look back at the past, we see that anxieties accompanied the run-up to every technological advance. In the nineteenth century, people believed that riding a train at more than 50 km/h was hazardous to their health; when machines began to enter factories, people were afraid that there would be no more work for them. Similarly, when the first personal computers appeared in offices and later the Internet and the New Economy transformed the business world. None of these fears have materialized, and the number of people employed and unemployed has remained largely unchanged. Thus, broadly speaking, the demand for human labor is much more dependent on the economy in general than on the aforementioned technological innovations.

References

Bartlett, A. (2006). The essential exponential! For the future of our planet. *Journal of Chemical Education, 83*. https://doi.org/10.1021/ed083p549.2

Doerr, J. (2018). *Why the secret to success is setting the right goals*. TED2018. Accessed December 1, 2021, from https://www.ted.com/talks/john_doerr_why_the_secret_to_success_is_setting_the_right_goals

Fortune. (2020). *Global 500*. Accessed December 1, 2021, from https://fortune.com/global500/

Gasteiger, J., & Zupan, J. (1999). *Neural networks in chemistry and drug design*. Wiley-VCH.

Kendall, K. (2020). *Photograph of a drone, Unsplash*. Accessed December 1, 2021, from https://unsplash.com/photos/6nRjHtBDk4o

Kraikivski, P. (2019). *Seeding the Singularity for AI*. arXiv preprint. Accessed December 1, 2021, from https://arxiv.org/abs/1908.01766

References

Obermaier, R. (Ed.). (2019). *Handbuch Industrie 4.0 und Digitale Transformation: Betriebswirtschaftliche, technische und rechtliche Herausforderungen*. Springer Gabler.

Reiss, S. (2004). Multifaceted nature of intrinsic motivation: The theory of 16 basic desires. *Review of General Psychology, 8*(3), 179–193. https://doi.org/10.1037/1089-2680.8.3.179

Schönert, W. (1996). *Werbung, die ankommt*. mi-Wirtschaftsbuch.

Statista. (2021). *Volumen der jährlich generierten/replizierten digitalen Datenmenge weltweit in den Jahren 2012 und 2020 und Prognose für 2025*. Accessed December 1, 2021, from https://de.statista.com/statistik/daten/studie/267974/umfrage/prognose-zum-weltweit-generierten-datenvolumen/

Turing, A. (1950). Computing machinery and intelligence. *Mind, 59*(236), 433–460.

Weizenbaum, J. (1966). ELIZA – A computer program for the study of natural language communication between man and machine. *Communications of the ACM, 9*, 36–45. https://doi.org/10.1145/365153.365168

Wergin, C. (2018). Unsere Daten haben Trumps Strategie bestimmt. *Die Welt online*. Accessed December 1, 2021, from https://www.welt.de/politik/ausland/article174785094/Cambridge-Analytica-Unsere-Daten-haben-Trumps-Strategie-bestimmt.html

GRANOBIZ: An Example from 2035

3

In order to illustrate the theoretical ideas presented here in a practical way, this chapter provides a concrete example of a self-driving company. The cereal bar manufacturer of the fictitious brand GRANOBIZ is used to show the many aspects of development from 2020 to 2035.

A classic organizational chart, as shown in Fig. 3.1, marks the beginning of this development. This evolved structure will be transformed into a new organizational chart in the ongoing evolution to a self-driving company qua agile company. The core of the self-organizing market research and product development team (previously: research and development) continues to consist of people who, based on their creativity, develop completely new, so-called disruptive products. These products are not to be understood as a linear further development of an existing product line. Disruptive means, for example, completely rethinking the relationship between company, product, and customer. In the area of muesli mixes, this has long been done within the framework of Industry 4.0; here, for example, customers can configure their own muesli online at "MyMuesli" (MyMüsli, 2020). Instead of buying a finished product, an automated form of an individual product is created here, which at the same time significantly increases customer loyalty.

GRANOBIZ goes one step further here and also enables individual packaging and choice of size. Using an intuitive user interface, the customer can put together their desired muesli chocolate bar. In 2035, this will be done with a balanced dose of additives, such as the entire spectrum of around 10,000 secondary plant substances as well as trace elements and vitamins. This means that the muesli bar will no longer just taste good. The bar for the mid-morning snack stimulates and invigorates the central nervous system, the one for afternoon sports contains, among other things, particularly high levels of magnesium, and the variant for later in the afternoon calms, relaxes, and ensures a restful sleep.

But even in the future, not all customers will want to configure their own bars. It can therefore be assumed that existing variants will also remain in the product line, especially because they can be positioned particularly well as agile digital brands

© The Author(s), under exclusive license to Springer-Verlag GmbH, DE, part of Springer Nature 2023
F. Schnitzhofer, *The Self-Driving Company*, Future of Business and Finance, https://doi.org/10.1007/978-3-662-68148-0_3

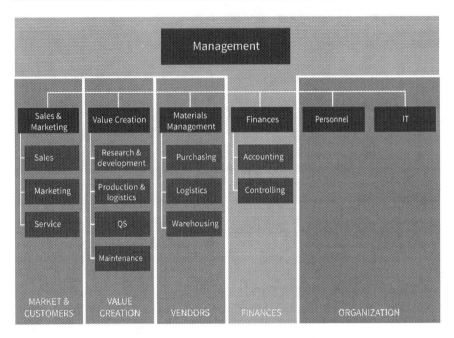

Fig. 3.1 Classical organizational chart of GRANOBIZ for 2000–2020

worldwide and tailored to the target group. Just as the Unilever Group's Magnum ice cream, for example, has been able to build up a strong brand personality, GRANOBIZ will also have such cash cows in its line of goods. These will adapt continuously and in a highly automated way to the most diversified needs of its most important customer groups worldwide.

For example, if there is feedback from a representative number of customers in Canada that the CrispyNut variant is a little too sweet, GRANOBIZ will immediately make an automated assessment. Since all company data is fully networked and immediately available, the algorithms networked for this purpose can immediately evaluate which of the following decisions is the most strategically target-oriented:

1. Product development: reduce the sugar content of CrispyNut by 7%
2. Diversify and develop a new variety, "CrispyNut vital"
3. Increase targeting of this customer cluster more with an existing, less sweet variety, for example, via a precisely targeted, automated ad campaign in Facebook

Larger decisions will still involve the product development team, with data presentation handled by the system. If necessary, this will involve a virtual team in several countries looking at this file, discussing it, developing new ideas and prototypes, testing them and, if appropriate, making the manual approval decision (see Fig. 3.2). The web store allows orders from the millions of individual customers and

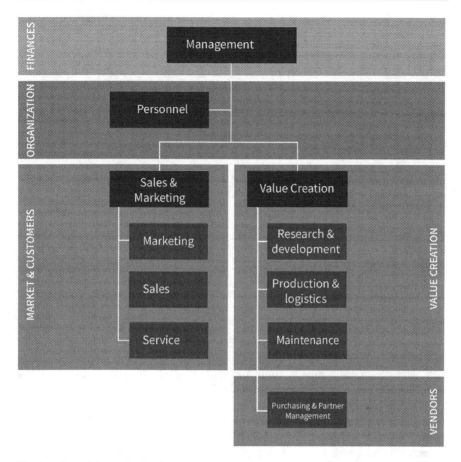

Fig. 3.2 Potential organizational chart of the self-driving company GRANOBIZ in 2035

middlemen distributed around the world to be placed fully automatically. In addition, a third software platform is used to organize the orders of the company's many suppliers and retailers in a fully automated manner. If the GRANOBIZ system orders oats from the mill, this is done via the platform. The new tenders for new series material, such as amaranth from South America, are also completely automated via the trading or contract platform (the former eProcurement platform). The system intelligently decides on the material to be procured and the ideal manufacturer or supplier. It handles all formalities, usually without the need for human intervention. For this reason, the system only cooperates with those suppliers who have also achieved a high level of digitization.

In the process, by 2035, a few global providers of trading platforms and contract platforms will have established themselves as providing smoothly functioning forms of collaboration, which will once again result in a significant increase in efficiency. These trading platforms are sales platforms for one side and eProcurement platforms for the other. The massive added value of these joint platforms lies in the automated exchange of order, delivery, and invoice data. This is because the third platform significantly reduces complexity that would otherwise have to be managed via a wide variety of individual interactions. The platform also significantly reduces financial transactions by eliminating the need to constantly allocate each partial payment back and forth. Rather, the system represents in real time the current status of multiple mutual credits or debits, which also has positive, international fiscal effects. In contrast to the tax tricks of the big corporations of the 2020s, the 2035 trading platform is based on a perceived fairness that can be achieved with absolute transparency of the system, even for small organic farmers.

Purchasing agents have long been a thing of the past. This task has been replaced by more exciting and meaningful work. At GRANOBIZ 2035, procurement means working with an international team to analyze long-term trends in the target countries using automatically processed metadata and, if appropriate, making necessary operational as well as long-term strategic decisions or developing creative new approaches. Active personal contact is maintained with the important major suppliers, and new ideas are constantly generated in the course of mutual discussions, which are then analyzed in terms of their feasibility.

Furthermore, the customer relationship is completely individualized in an automated way. GRANOBIZ knows each individual customer, knows their preferences and knows, for instance, that Marie-Luise Müller prefers certain customized high-protein sport bars and in what quantity she consumes them. From this, automated conclusions are drawn in the company about future behavior and thus also about future production. If behavior suddenly changes because Ms. Müller has hurt herself while working out, the company can also react quickly to this situation and, in a needs-oriented dialog with Ms. Müller, suggest the "CuraBar" variant that supports regeneration particularly well. In this way, customers receive support over many years. At 18, they are still going to the gym to build up muscles, then they gradually shift their activities more towards the outdoors and mountain biking, and later they start Nordic walking. GRANOBIZ 2035 sees itself as a personal coach and trainer who accompanies its customers throughout their lives and offers the right nutritional supplement for every situation. GRANOBIZ does this job not only for all of Mrs. Müller's cherished needs, but for millions of customers worldwide, with its algorithms always affording the highest possible quality.

In the B2B area, GRANOBIZ tracks important market partners, such as fitness studios. Since all data on user behavior is available, there is an excellent basis for deploying people here and establishing personal contacts with the operators of the studio chains. In the case of important key accounts, therefore, personal talks, relationship building, and trust will continue to play the decisive role. The role of the sales representative will be more highly valued, as they will have all the data they need to achieve a positive buying decision on the part of the client. Intelligent sales software will coordinate all the details of the meeting, set the agenda, and provide supporting marketing materials for the conversation at the exactly right place. Even a "script" for the successful closing of the sale has been prepared by the AI-based software as well as a corresponding response to potential objections. Thus, a deal is

3 GRANOBIZ: An Example from 2035

reached and the generated data of the sales meeting flow back into the sales software for future improvements. In addition, the successful closing triggers relevant activities at GRANOBIZ in real time. Production is scheduled and logistics and shipping are prepared—again, all in a fully automated fashion.

People will also continue to play a decisive role in new products. As before, the new bars are personally appraised and sampled. GRANOBIZ can afford a food scout because of its good profit margins. The biologist, ethnologist, and star chef travels all over the world and stays for weeks with indigenous peoples, intensively studying eating habits that have evolved over thousands of years. He or she roams the jungle with the indigenous, finds nuts, fruits, and roots with outstanding properties that have not yet been used in any cuisine in the world. Based on current laboratory studies, these substances are cleared and go into new products. Exciting workshops are held in the company's experimental kitchen. Together with the CEO, the head of marketing, and the heads of product development and market research, they chop, slice, stir, bake, and fry until a bar is created that the world has never seen or tasted before. After the prototype has been successfully tested, the system resumes further production, marketing, and distribution completely on its own. This example gives a good indication of how the self-driving company will generate unplanned new roles, titles, and jobs.

Time and again, at informal meetings in the outdoor garden of the company cafeteria, people tell each other the old stories from the 2020s, when 95% of the day still consisted of paralyzing PC work, when they went home with headaches and neck pain, and were so empty inside that the only small consolation was an evening in front of the TV or a Netflix series. Yet everyone had thought they were so cutting-edge. People had looked down on the assembly line workers of the nineteenth and early twentieth centuries who had to eke out their existence in miserable conditions with eternally identical hand motions at the machine—without realizing that by the 2020s, the partially digitized company had merely replaced monotonous physical labor with monotonous mental labor.

Bruno Kreisky recognized as early as the 1970s that "[a]n intelligent person works playfully." Unfortunately, at that time only a few people were granted the opportunity to work in a truly intelligent manner within the company; ultimately, this was reserved for the top executives. Anyone who brought in too many new ideas was considered a disruptive force and dangerous. They were either forced to "work according to the book" or dismissed altogether. "We do things here the way we've always done them." It is astonishing how long this form of work organization was able to survive.

GRANOBIZ orders go into the warehouse in real time, with not a single person driving around a forklift since the complex, highly flexible, high-tech facility was built. Meanwhile, old stories are told, like that of the alcohol prevention program that tried to keep warehouse workers away from addiction. Still, accidents and serious injuries kept happening because forklift drivers kept the flask well hidden.

At GRANOBIZ, there is no longer an annual inventory, since the system of the self-driving organization with real-time inventory continuously has the data on current ACTUAL and TARGET status and immediately initiates all necessary measures, such as orders from suppliers. These are also already highly automated, which means that human intervention is no longer required on this side either, based on the existing supply contract. Whereas in the past there were still entry or transmission errors or loss of documents when the wind blew in through an open office window, in 2035 the software works completely error-free. This is because it is networked in a complex manner throughout the entire company, and every slightest deviation in this overall organism is immediately recorded and corrected without the controlling department having to assign an employee to it.

Anyone who has ever had to calculate a logistics task in mathematics knows that optimized logistics offers considerable potential for savings. A common example is the company with several offices and production facilities spread across its premises; a diagram captures these units in their exact dimensions. This is combined with the number of employees in the individual production facilities. The question now posed: where on the site should the company canteen best be located? The failure rates in leaving exams in mathematics, especially for such written tasks, show just how poorly suited most people are at solving such problems. For the algorithms in self-driving companies, this problem is solved in less than a nanosecond. Moreover, logistics are not calculated for a specific state alone, instead the solutions are in a constant state of flux, with the individual parameters, such as the location and quantity of the respective products or raw materials, constantly exchanging information with each other about their current status.

In this way, the warehouse in the self-driving company of 2035 functions comparably to an ant colony: Here, evolution already ensured 130 million years ago the building of a complex, decentralized information system. It has brought about the highest efficiency and the outstanding success of this species up to the present day: despite the population explosion, there is still more biomass in the form of ants than of humans on this planet. Briefly explained: Every ant leaves behind information on its incessant paths in the form of scent trails, for instance, about enemies, building material, or food sources. If an ant crosses a path, it receives the information that it must turn right and that the delicious carcass of a butterfly larva is located there at a distance of about 2.5 m, which is to be transported off to the burrow in a joint effort. The direction can be recognized by the second ant by the strength of the scent. In the concrete case, the scent is stronger to the left, where the information-giving ant has moved to—therefore the other ant knows that it has to go to the right. Anyone who as a child lying on its stomach in the garden has observed ants can certainly remember that the animals have a peculiar angular form of locomotion. Today we understand this perfectly. As in a network of algorithms, a complex network of current information is thus created in the ant colony, in which exactly those ants that are on the spot immediately carry out the correct task in the interest of the well-being of the colony as a whole.

If the same ant, as is the case in today's analog companies, would first have to walk the long distance to the burrow, endless processes would be necessary to enable the transport of the fat butterfly larva. First, the ant would have to find the responsible boss, a difficult task with several thousand workers. Then the situation would have to be discussed and a new search would begin to organize the right transport ants.

When they finally arrive at the presumed location, after having lost their way several times, the larva would have long since disappeared, having been eaten in the meantime by a crow.

With such an organizational system, ants would have long since gone extinct. Interestingly, in 2020, most companies still operate on this—essentially primitive—centralized basis. When the ants developed their "self-driving" ecosystem 150 million years ago, they were so successful that in the meantime many other insect species have come—and gone again. The question that now arises is how many of the world's analog companies will still exist in 2035.

Shipping is just as fully automated as warehouse logistics, whereby GRANOBIZ cooperates with partner companies that are also highly self-driving. All the other companies have by now lost their orders because their interface management could not be fully digitized. Many years ago, there was still an interface with which suppliers could enter their data manually or scan freight documents. This device is now in the company museum.

Reference

MyMüsli. (2020). *Muesli Mixer.* Accessed December 1, 2021, from https://www.mymuesli.com/mixer/

Digitization and Technical Word Bingo

4

As an experienced software strategy consultant, for years I have repeatedly seen projects that do not work at all in large and successful companies. One example that illustrates this well is the app for buying a ticket from a public transport provider. The idea behind this principle is quite simple: it should enable users to search for a suitable connection on their cell phone and pay for the ticket with a click. The result: the app cost the transport company over 100 million euros—while an average app with similar functionality would cost around 70,000 €. What went wrong here?

This project was based on a particularly high level of software complexity due to the existing systems. The new system had to be built on top of five large and countless small existing software apps. In principle this alone need not to have been so bad: it would cost about five times as much, that is, about 350,000 €. Even if the connection of only one of these large existing apps would have cost about one million euros, that would only be five million euros in total, and thus still far from 100 million. So where did the remaining millions go? Why can a "simple" software project generate such exorbitant costs?

The complexity drivers in this project were the existing apps and political power-driven ambitions within the company. First of all, it is important to know that the transport operator had numerous existing software programs. These were classically evolved and outdated backend systems, developed with decades-old programming languages. Additional complexity was caused by the cross-border character of the transport services, since all international connections and data also had to be taken into account, thus necessitating further interfaces. Each of the major existing applications was assigned to a subdivision within the company and was the responsibility of a department manager. Each of these managers had different ideas and did not really act in concert. Instead of setting up the entire system from scratch, the new system was built, with a high degree of complexity, on top of the mess of existing systems. In addition to the enormous integration effort, the power structure in the project was also far too complex. The size of the project, the complexity of the technical solution, and the multitude of different external and internal implementers

© The Author(s), under exclusive license to Springer-Verlag GmbH, DE, part of Springer Nature 2023
F. Schnitzhofer, *The Self-Driving Company*, Future of Business and Finance,
https://doi.org/10.1007/978-3-662-68148-0_4

and their interests caused these high costs. The outcome of the project is an overpriced, error-prone app that is not intuitive to use, has many bugs, and to top it all off, is too slow to use.

A similar problem plagues almost all banks today, the basic software structures of which are also outdated. These companies maintain IT & software departments with several hundred employees so that new applications can be built around these ancient systems. Of course, in order to manage these employees, an additional 10% or so of middle and senior managers is required. For a 700-person software department, this means 65–75 managers. Hundreds of meetings are required each year to coordinate with the various specialized departments. To start any fundamental new process often requires 3 years of labor-intensive work with extremely high wage costs.

In addition, there is often considerable resistance from the users. People are creatures of habit as are many employees. They have paradoxically grown fond of their old software with the DOS input window and are not at all willing to consider letting go and opening themselves to new solutions. In sum, it is a broad mass that exerts considerable resistance to software projects.

The path to true self-driving companies is only possible if these outdated systems are radically modernized. As the examples have shown, attempts to build on top of legacy systems cause higher costs in the long run than the fundamental renewal of the entire software. While new company buildings are being erected and the vehicle fleet is being replaced, savings are supposedly being made in software by preserving "that which has proven its worth"—precisely in an area where modernization is proceeding particularly rapidly.

This is where the term "technical debt" comes in. Whether it's building technology, vehicles, or software, any technical system in which investments are not made on an ongoing basis accumulates technical debt. If my car is not serviced regularly, I will soon have to expect higher repair costs because, for example, the engine has been damaged due to lack of lubrication. As a rule, it can be assumed that about 15%–20% of the initial project value ("set-up costs") must be invested in ongoing improvements and renewals—known as "refactoring" in technical jargon—in order to avoid accumulating technical debt. If this does not take place, one will have to pay for this debt at some point. Especially in the software area, many companies including large corporations have failed to do this in recent decades. In their "underbellies" they carry around enormous technical debt in the form of inhomogeneous systems.

Another example from the banking industry: The most important core banking applications of a majority of the system-relevant banks in Europe were written with the COBOL programming language or related programming languages from the 1950s. The technology behind the COBOL programming language is an evolutionary step further development based on the old punch card system. Punch cards are simple programs and were historically developed to operate mechanical looms. So the banks are working with a three-tiered system based on technology one evolutionary step further development old mechanical looms. And now they are trying to appear worldly, modern, and omni-channel to the outside world. This means that

4 Digitization and Technical Word Bingo

every prospect and customer, no matter what channel he or she uses, always has the same business opportunities and always receives the same information. Whether it's via data glasses, WhatsApp, mobile app, website, phone, or over the counter. To date, about 80% of all banks still make use of this legacy system. It is easy to understand that this cannot generate a high level of agility. The path to a truly modernized system can therefore only be taken if this foundation is completely revamped. Even though all top managers ultimately want to get there, no one has yet been willing to take this decisive step.

Apart from the future vision of the self-driving company, this means that many basic functions that should be standard today are not possible or only possible to a limited extent. It should have long been a matter of course to know about all customer interactions everywhere in the company and to be able to react accordingly. Why does this still not work today? Why are IT and software projects always doomed to fail and exceed all time and cost targets? Here are some reasons:

- Because of the extreme level of accumulated technical debt: The projects have reached a size and complexity that enormously increases the risk of failure. It is difficult to coordinate 100 creative experts in such a large project in a way that produces effective output.
- During the rebuild phase, the requirements for the existing systems are constantly changing, yet these systems must continue to function in some form—it is as if a house were being rebuilt and at the same time had to be continuously inhabited by all of its inhabitants.
- The influence of power politics at the middle management level in large companies usually makes system requirements too complex and impossible to implement in a meaningful way. Moreover, these requirements are often not articulated until the implementation phase, bringing even well-managed projects to the brink of failure.
- The methods for creating and integrating software have improved significantly over the last 50 years, yet my experience shows that more than 80% of industrially produced software projects are estimated incorrectly. This erroneous estimation of the time required and the resulting costs even before the start of a project damages the reputation of an entire industry. Most of the time the estimates are 40–50% below the actual time and effort needed. My experience shows that these projects are usually not implemented if the correct costs are communicated to the decision-makers in advance. This all starts, or at least should, with the proper development of a business case for the entire life cycle of a given piece of software.
- Business-critical software—especially at the backend—usually has a life cycle of 15–20 years. For instance, even the major vendors of ERP systems bring out a release every 15–20 years.

While there is a technical inspection report for all kinds of technical devices, this does not exist in the area of software, even though it carries an extremely high technical responsibility for the functioning of entire industries. At the same time, this also means that everything that takes place using this software should be 100% comprehensible and documentable. Whereas the cars in the fleet are supplied with the latest inspection stickers, software processes are still in operation in the company that have long since become hopelessly outdated. Because this has simply been the case for too long, there is little awareness of, or expertise about, this problem in the company.

Every decision-maker is fully aware that a highly safe, self-driving car cannot be built on the basis of a 1956 VW Beetle. However, this understanding does not exist for software solutions.

4.1 Setup of Complex Software Projects

The basis of every industrialized software project is the initial cost estimate. For this purpose, resources have to be planned, costs have to be estimated, and milestones have to be defined up to the end of the project. From the beginning of software development, the programming performance of software has been evaluated with metrics. Person days (PT), lines of code (LOC), story points (SP), or price of service per programming hour (€) were used. All of these metrics provide only a limited indication of objective programming performance or the actual scope of the software purchased or programmed.

Current productivity factors are mostly subjective and especially for purchased programming services it is difficult to compare vendors. There is a need for simple and standardized metrics to estimate development performance. The following sections describe ways to accurately estimate costs from the very outset of a software project.

4.1.1 Comparative Estimates

In agile software development projects especially the initial cost estimate poses new challenges for managers. Practice shows that in the majority of such projects, the complete project scope has not yet been conclusively defined at the beginning of the project. In these situations, comparative estimates are then made: "Presumably, this project is of comparable size to project XY and will therefore cost about 2 million euros." This represents a simple estimation method that can be used to define a rough budgetary framework. In the next project phase, this estimate has to be fleshed out. As a preliminary step, the actual specialized, functional scope of the project with all its high-level use cases (= epics) has to be defined. Only in this way can a reliable cost estimate be made.

Different methods exist for estimating costs; these can be selected and combined depending on the project situation. For a correct cost estimate, it should be noted that the numerical value is always provided with a certain level of imprecision (variance). Many years of experience with estimates have shown that they rarely deviate downwards. In the majority of software projects, the actual implementation costs are significantly higher than the initial estimate. In the rough estimate of a project, the deviation can be up to 40% of the initial value estimated. The accuracy of detailed estimate (bottom-up estimate) of a software project should be within the 20% range of the actual implementation costs.

4.1.2 Expert Estimates

Depending on the complexity, priority, and size of a project, different methods of estimate by experts are used. The simplest estimation methodology involves the estimate by an exceptionally experienced senior project manager. Due to the numerous software projects he or she has completed, this expert is able to estimate—with little effort—the specific expenditures required by the various project participants. The larger the projects become, the more important multiple expert estimates become in order to bring different perspectives into the estimation procedure.

4.1.3 Estimates Made by the Development Team

Modern software development teams tend to use easily comprehensible assessments of the technical implementation complexity of requirements. The complexity assessment results are therefore presented in the form of "story points," T-shirt sizes (S, M, L, XL, XXL), or other size groupings (e.g., large buildings, superhero strengths, . . .). Based on historical experience, this complexity estimate can be used to infer the actual implementation costs. In general, complex mathematical models for calculating costs should be avoided, as they provide a deceptive degree of certainty. This is because it only takes one incorrectly estimated factor to completely distort these results.

The most cost-effective and objective method is based on a simple calculation (e.g., 1 can implement a Story Point with the cost of 2 person days). In this way, implementation costs can be inferred from complexity.

4.2 The Monolithic Heart: Enterprise Resource Planning

With the introduction of Enterprise Resource Planning (ERP) systems, companies began to implant a kind of monolithic software heart, storing all the data they needed to perform their activities: incoming invoices, outgoing invoices, inventory, production or logistics data. In this way, all end-to-end processes in the company are covered. At the same time, the introduction of these ERP systems has created a very high level of standardization in these companies. This was necessary because there are a large number of standard topics that need to be introduced in the company as part of an ERP migration. For example, if the company buys a simple iPad, it needs a requisition for it—that is, a cost center, a quote, a purchase order, a delivery, and an invoice, the amount of which is then transferred to the retailer via a bank and

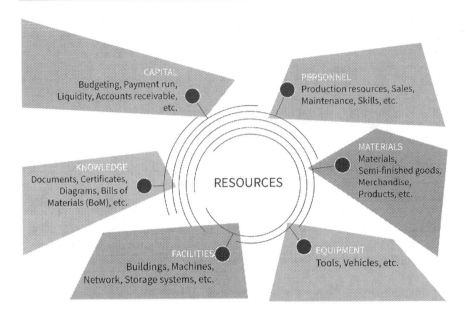

Fig. 4.1 Managed resources of an enterprise resource planning (ERP) system

subsequently written off against taxes when the quarterly statement is issued. An ERP system is used to manage and plan the resources in a company. These resources include capital, personnel, knowledge, materials, equipment, operating resources, and much more (see Fig. 4.1).

Before the introduction of these ERP systems, these subprocesses were still carried out by hand and often in a very casual manner. Erroneous orders occurred, deliveries were accepted that had never been ordered, invoices were overlooked or lost. In the meantime, the companies have been conditioned by the precise specifications of the system to such an extent that the processes run largely correctly—and the higher the level of digitization, the better.

Nevertheless, two further important steps are still missing on the road to the self-driving company of 2035. Once all subprocesses have been largely standardized and digitized, real-time accounting has been achieved. With such accounting, the current financial status of the company can be called up at any time at the push of a button. It would therefore no longer be necessary to painstakingly prepare an annual financial statement; instead, the results of the last 12 months could also be determined and compared quite simply and at any time. However, software companies such as SAP, Oracle, or Microsoft are not quite up to this yet, even SAP's new S/4Hana is not yet able to do this.

Why is this not yet possible? The software companies approach the problem too technocratically, while the entrepreneurs are used to the existing procedure, do not question it, and therefore do not push ahead with this decisive change. The entrepreneurs believe that by looking at the quarterly figures and the current account balance, they can get a good intuitive assessment of the situation and make any given

4.2 The Monolithic Heart: Enterprise Resource Planning

decision on this basis. If these decisions result in unfavorable developments, another reason is always found for this, which lies outside the entrepreneur's own responsibility: it is claimed that the market is developing badly (without concrete data to show this), the customers are unsettled because of the competition, the products have qualitative problems, or seasonal effects are suspected.

This leaves possible self-inflicted errors undetected, for instance, in estimating liquidity—even though research in the field of behavioral economics has long since shown the wide variety of errors that people make in such estimations. In view of open outgoing invoices with undetermined payment, accounting gaps due to arrears payments for social security and income tax, and countless small supplier liabilities, this is easy to understand.

In purely theoretical terms, all of these subprocesses are already predefined once the decision is made to engage a particular vendor: delivery, invoice, payment, tax claim. When the order is entered, for example, the system already knows whether and to what extent this item can be written off. This means that the entire process chain is already available in bundled form at this moment. This also applies to all other decisions in the entire system, allowing the overall financial situation to be captured in a matter of seconds or called up on request.

In the future, the calculation of this overall result will therefore be more like a share price than an annual report. The current EBIT (earnings before interest and taxes) will be visible in real time, and at the push of a button it will be possible in 2035 to obtain a forecast in any time window based on past performance. So when an iPad is purchased, the company will know in real time the effect of the tax write-off it triggers and will therefore be able to make a precise forecast.

It is also highly unlikely that a newcomer will enter the market offering this total solution. It would be as if a vendor were to enter the market proposing to completely resurface all roads with something other than asphalt—in other words, to completely change an existing infrastructure that is widely used around the world in just a few years. In the same way, the existing ERP infrastructures of SAP, Oracle, Microsoft, and Sage have been established for decades and are a fixed component of most companies that is difficult to change.

If we now assume that we have access to all data in real time—purchasing, inventory, supplier invoices, personnel costs, share of fixed costs, future tax and social security effects, and so on—and can generate a forecast just as quickly, we have a basis for making all operational, as well as tactical, decisions fully automatically and executing them through machines. If a vehicle manufacturer signs a contract with a steel mill to produce 1.2 million vehicles in the following year, all the resulting operational and tactical decisions can in turn be made at the steel mill to produce this quantity of steel sheet coils in the desired quality and deliver them on time.

An important area of development for ERP systems or upstream expert systems will be the strategic and tactical support of management decisions. While many operational decisions are already automated to a high degree, tactical decisions are still made by humans in middle management. Here, mistakes occur again and again, often because the decisions are not exactly aligned with the strategy, or this strategy is based on insufficient or misinterpreted data. Strategies today are therefore still not sufficiently data-driven. For example, when a service company realizes that its margin is too low, it tries to increase the price of its services, but without being able to calculate exactly what impact this will have on demand.

In the future, it will be possible to perform the simulations required for strategy in unprecedented quality and at any desired point in time. For example, it will be possible to create precise simulations of the scenarios that will occur as a result of a price increase based on all the effects it triggers. So while work in this area is still predominantly analog and takes place in meetings with controversial, emotional discussions and flip charts, strategic decisions in the future will be increasingly data-driven.

Until the early 2000s, reasonably reliable 3- to 5-year plans were still created on this analog basis. Since then, the speed of change in general conditions has increased enormously. And the preparation of the underlying data has not been able to keep up with this speed. Therefore, in recent years, it has become increasingly difficult for many companies to develop strategies for this kind of time window. Accordingly, strategies have become more and more short term, but also more and more short-sighted, following the motto: "if a hole opens, close it." With the focus on these hectic short-term decisions, however, the indispensable long-term vision has been lost. Thus, many companies have not recognized and still do not recognize that their software structures and subsystems are hopelessly outdated and unfit for the future. Only a look at the years 2030 and beyond enables meaningful strategic planning. Hence the vision of the self-driving company.

4.3 The Customer Is King: Customer Relationship Management

Customer Relationship Management (CRM) systems are one of the most important technological components of the self-driving company. These systems contain all the information about prospective customers—potential and real, as well as active and former customers. In addition, these systems combine the view of the market and customer groups.

Future systems will only be the same as today's systems in terms of their foundation. However, the range of functions will increase many times over. In addition, the data hunger of these systems will increase massively. While up to now only the most important company and contact master data, communications, sales conversations (sales leads), and sales opportunities have been stored in it, in the future information about market groups, market trends, potential customers, and all available information about them will be stored in the CRM.

A CRM system consists of three components: First, it reflects a company's view of the market. All activities related to traditional as well as future marketing will be implementable with this part of the system. The second part deals with the classic sales process and ranges from the first contact to the completion of the contract. In the third part, these systems deal with existing customers and their additional

4.3 The Customer Is King: Customer Relationship Management

purchasing wishes, their complaints, and service requests. Thus, these systems cover the complete life cycle of a customer in the company.

The manufacturers of the leading CRM systems are already preparing for the post-automation phase. For example, the initial attempts at AI algorithms are already being incorporated today. However, it will probably take until after 2027 before all the functions needed for a self-driving company are implemented. The leading manufacturers of CRM systems today are Salesforce, Microsoft, Hubspot, and a large number of individual manufacturers of special and industry solutions.

If you now look at the part of a CRM system directed towards the market, you will notice that basic functionality still needs to be implemented. It is important for the correct penetration of the market that the responsible department is provided with all information about its potential target groups. It wants to select the target group it seeks to address. Of course, this selection process will continue to be a human task and people will also select the content and target of their communication. The software system will then add the concrete design, graphics, and follow-on sources. In addition, the CRM system will select from the available marketing channels, the right one for the right person. For example, the system will independently recognize whether a potential customer is better reached via a video on Netflix or, instead, via an ad placed in his or her favorite online science magazine. The system dynamically decides which channels to use. If the systems of Google Analytics, LinkedIn, Xing, Facebook, and the many other channels are not yet directly integrated with a CRM system today, one can expect this integration work to be completed by 2025. These new channels to customers can be compared to the advent of email at the turn of the millennium. For the next 5–10 years, they will represent one of the most important methods for generating leads. After that, the volume of spam will reach similar dimensions and sales approaches via these media will no longer be possible.

In addition, a CRM system will provide companies with more options for sending information to potential customer groups. Today, we use static newsletter systems for this purpose, but in a few years, this technology will also undergo massive development. There will be a move away from the hard-coded timing of sending flat information texts to all addressees via email. In the future, individualized information will be sent to potential customers via a wide variety of channels. The time of sending will vary from channel to channel and will be based on the likelihood that this information will actually be read and digested. Time, content, medium, and communication channel are each selected according to sales probability and the information is sent in a targeted manner.

In the process, all relevant data on viewing, usage, and buying behavior are fed back into the CRM. These methods provide companies with increasingly improved insights into target and customer groups. In contrast to today, these insights are not stored at the group level, but at the individual level. Moreover, this collected data can be used for the entire sales process and over the entire life cycle of any given customer.

4.4 Automation Through Software Robots

Robotic process automation (RPA)—that is, software robotics—is a topic that is receiving increasing attention. Process and procedure automation accompany companies and organizations on their way to digitization and increase their competitiveness on the market through more efficient and faster process flows. However, employees and staff are often skeptical about the topic, since, for one thing, they are fearful of losing their jobs. This makes it more difficult to introduce this technology in businesses. More generally, it represents a kind of transitional technology on the road to the self-driving company, which is necessary until the old software connected to it is replaced by new, fully autonomous systems. Thus, especially for larger companies that have evolved over decades, RPA will be particularly important in the coming years.

Software robots are applications that mimic human interaction with the user interfaces of software systems and perform functions autonomously in this way. RPA technology is the fastest growing segment in the global software market. The largest users of RPA continue to be banks, insurance companies, and telecommunication companies, as these often have legacy systems in use, the replacement of which is associated with enormous effort and considerable expense. In such cases, RPA takes on an important interface function, for example, for transferring data from these legacy systems to new systems. RPA represents a bridge technology that provides the benefits of digitization at an early stage and financially supports the replacement of obsolete systems in the medium term. Large software companies such as Microsoft, IBM and SAP have also recognized the potential that RPA brings. They have begun to enter into partnerships with RPA providers or to buy them up in order to integrate their services into their solutions. This fact contributes to a further increase in awareness and acceptance of RPA in the market.

The use of RPA brings significant benefits to a company or organization. To integrate an RPA tool into a company or organization, there is no need to change the existing system landscape. The RPA software coexists and interacts with existing systems—hence its suitability as a transitional solution for large software replacement projects, as the technology allows data to be transferred between two or more systems without having to implement a complicated interface to do so. Since the installation of RPA tools is usually rapid and the automation of processes can be started quickly, a quick return on investment can often be achieved. Depending on the complexity of the process and the know-how or skills of the person automating it, automation of simple processes, including testing, can take as little as a few weeks.

Employees can be relieved of repetitive and long-winded processes by automating them, allowing these members of the workforce to devote themselves to more demanding tasks, such as improving the customer experience. The keyword is quality improvement: this is achieved by, for example, reducing the number of erroneous entries caused by humans, and thus lowering operational risk. In addition, automated processes can be executed more often as well as overnight or over the weekend. For instance, the robot could prepare an elaborate report every night, which serves to minimize risk—whereas, due to lack of time, an employee could

4.4 Automation Through Software Robots

only deal with the issue once a week. Another advantage is the optimization of existing processes, which goes hand in hand with the use of RPA. The processes to be automated are thoroughly analyzed and documented prior to the automation phase. The chance that optimization potential will be uncovered here is high since an intensive examination of processes takes place that may not have been scrutinized for many years. The more efficiently a process is designed in the documentation phase, the faster and more efficiently the automated function will run.

The most important suitability criteria for processes that can be automated are based on the fact that they are rule-based and standardized. By means of RPA tools, most work steps that are still carried out by employees at great expense on a laptop or PC can be automated. Examples of activities that can be automated are mouse clicks, copy and paste activities, filling fields, comparing values or tables, or searching texts for specific values. There are processes that are more suitable for automation than others. Processes suitable for automation are based on defined rules and are therefore repeatable. They follow a defined structure and contain relatively few exceptions. Processes are unsuitable for automation if they are based on human decisions and contain a large number of variants, ramifications, and exceptions. Equally unsuitable are processes in which contact with humans generally plays a role, since software robots cannot react flexibly to input in the same way that artificial intelligence can and only strictly follow the designed automated process flow.

In addition, customers usually prefer contact with real people rather than robots. Moreover, before automating a process, one must always ask whether the process can be optimized or automated in another way. For example, processes that are heavily Excel-based could also be carried out by using macros. Processes that can be automated can usually be found in all departments or divisions of a company or organization. An example of an application in IT would be the setup of a new user; in finance and controlling, the preparation of reports from SAP tables, for example, can be automated. The updating of personnel data or the processing of vacation requests are, for example, applications from HR (human resources).

Close cooperation between business and IT is essential in the area of RPA. In most cases, the organizational units and business departments provide the processes, document them, and hand over the documentation along with suitable test data to IT for the implementation and testing of the automated process. Depending on the RPA governance model, it is also possible for IT to provide an RPA platform and for organizational units to perform the automation processes themselves. Usually, however, the automation processes take place in a centralized manner in one department (usually IT) in order to avoid a proliferation of different automated processes in the organization. Moreover, the process must be regularly maintained and adjusted after automation if changes occur in the process flow. Setting up a suitable communication channel between organizational units and IT is of great importance here in order to maintain the quality of the automated processes and avoid errors at an early stage.

As the discussion has shown, RPA is still based on the "old" linear, end-to-end processes, which will, however, be replaced in the long term by autonomous software algorithms and artificial intelligence. Nevertheless, they are often indispensable in the transitional phase. They also have an important advantage in that they provide a good basis for analyzing the existing structure and pinpointing many of its weak points.

4.5 The Architecture of Company Software

Just as a house is built from bricks, concrete, and mortar, the self-driving company will be constructed from individual software solutions, network connections, and databases. To stay with the analogy of building a house, the term architecture can also be used here as a constructive and planning element. In the case of the self-running company, this term refers to the enterprise architecture. It describes the interaction of all IT and software solutions in a company. A well-planned enterprise-wide architecture must be created from structures that have developed over time. In this the integration of these software solutions, data transfer, and data storage play a central role. Here too, architecture is not an end in itself, but must be tailored to the needs of the company and its markets. Reaching the highest level of a self-driving company requires sophisticated architectonic planning of all existing and future IT and software solutions.

Enterprise software architecture serves as the connecting structure that binds all areas of the self-driving company together. Omnichannel architecture plays an important role in this context. It allows customers to approach the company with their diverse concerns via any channel and be satisfied in the same high-quality way. Providing this level of services, however, creates major problems for many companies today. For example, it should be possible to open a bank account directly via WhatsApp and receive all the information needed there and, at the same time, have all the information about the person opening the account stored in the bank. Often, customer software systems are only isolated solutions that are very well accepted and used by customers, but are not integrated into an overall architecture in the company.

The challenge for all systems that interact with people and especially with customers is that their lifespan is limited to about 3–5 years. Classic websites are the best examples of this. Here, the demands on design and usability change so frequently that they have to be updated and reprogrammed every few years. In the case of mobile applications and customer portals, too, technological progress is advancing so rapidly that a complete overhaul has to be considered every few years. If you now combine this fact with the classic life cycles of 15–25 years for central software systems, you are looking at a world of systems at two different speeds. This fact leads to special challenges in software architecture. Central enterprise functionalities of the software systems must be made available as standardized services for the long term. Customer-oriented software applications integrate these services and thus build on the data and functions of the back-end systems. This service layer serves as a coupling between the layers that are developing at different speeds.

4.5 The Architecture of Company Software

Another trend in software architecture is the use of standardized software containers. Here software development has borrowed from modern shipping with its standardized containers. The advantage of this is that these standardized containers can be "loaded" anywhere with minimal effort. In the case of software, this means that the software is installed in a container and this container is operated on a server. Thus, the server is our container ship, and the software is the cargo content of a standardized container. Similar to shipping, moving active software from one server to another is therefore child's play. The use of software containers is already standard, especially for cloud-based services.

The large core business applications serve as the basis for all corporate functions. In many large companies, these are still monolithic, outdated software applications. It is not uncommon for them to be 30 or more years old, and numerous auxiliary software solutions and other technical crutches have developed around these applications to ensure the smooth use of functions and data. Especially for these areas, an enterprise software architecture that is well planned for the long term is of great importance.

Even if, from my own practical experience, some very important software applications have been in smooth operation for far longer than 40 years, companies have to ask themselves whether they want to build a self-driving company on top of these outdated and encrusted structures. In fact, this won't work anyway. The big challenge in this area is to find combinations of standard software applications—such as ERP systems—and individually developed special solutions that give a company that essential unique selling point or proposition (USP). The foundation of a self-driving company will almost certainly be standard software solutions. Its USP can only be achieved through special integration or through unique individual software solutions.

Essential for achieving a self-driving company is also the company-wide knowledge of all available databases. All individual systems must be aware of and have access to all available data. The processing of data is based on this simple rule: each data object managed by a single company must be able to be created, read, updated, searched, and deleted by all the other software solutions in the company. This is also referred to as the CRUDS principle: create, read, update, delete, and search.

In addition, data sinks must be established in order to quickly gain an overview of all existing data using data analysis tools. Furthermore, learning algorithms are based on the optimized use of historical data. Thus, there must exist a semantic meta-model for understanding all data that can be processed by the system. Much of the crucial development will take place in this area over the next decade. Based on our experience, it is in the large companies that we find the greatest need to catch up in this area.

Practice shows that enterprise software architecture should not be an academic exercise. On the contrary, one must pragmatically compare a company's current status with its desired goal and work out a long-term plan for sustainable development. Again, a 15-year plan must be followed. The biggest misunderstanding in this discipline is about the time frame of planning, which is very often seen only over a 3- to 5-year period. However, the key to success lies in taking a 10- to 20-year time frame into consideration. In addition, accompanying dimensions such as the operation and development of software must also be considered. The central element of software architecture is the consideration of the entire life cycle of all applications and the way they interact. As the discussion in this chapter shows, a well-planned enterprise software architecture must be launched today in order to successfully exploit by 2035 all the potentials for establishing a self-driving company.

Problem Areas in Analog Companies

5

This chapter presents the currently prevailing "business theory", which has evolved over decades, but has remained unchanged, since to date only partial digitization has taken place in almost all companies, based on the old, "analog" structures.

The structure of the ensuing discussions is based on the most important corporate process groups, which are representative of a widespread approach to the structuring of processes in companies. To date, therefore, digitization has been carried out on the basis of traditional analog end-to-end processes instead of, conversely, thinking about digitization from the considerably more far-reaching opportunities afforded by artificial intelligence (see Fig. 5.1).

First, the problem areas are described and illustrated with examples. On the basis of this understanding, a description is given of the enormous potentials that could be unleashed in companies if they are courageous enough to embark on the path of becoming self-driving companies. In this context, it will also be shown how process-oriented operational and organizational structures will soon be history once fully networked algorithms communicating in real time take over 80% of all functions and establish a completely new generation of performance with operational and tactical decisions based on the complete range of real-time information.

This also demonstrates how the rigid boundaries of departments limit people's thinking and, on the basis of isolated "inside-the-box" thinking, hinder the achievement of the overall company optimum in the daily rush for one's own advantage. We will outline how the new total organism will result in the overcoming of this restricted thinking—and through the completely new opportunities arising from the alleviation of routines, a new holistic view of the company will also make its breakthrough.

This development is comparable to the automobile, which for a century has been thought of and built around the engine. This core element and its hundreds of components have been developed and researched for decades—just as the core processes of companies are still being tinkered with today in order to achieve a few percent more efficiency—instead of seeing the much greater untapped potential

---

© The Author(s), under exclusive license to Springer-Verlag GmbH, DE, part of Springer Nature 2023
F. Schnitzhofer, *The Self-Driving Company*, Future of Business and Finance,
https://doi.org/10.1007/978-3-662-68148-0_5

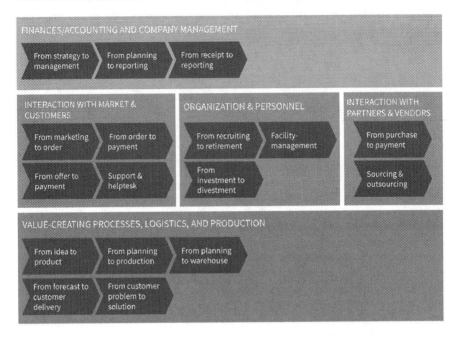

Fig. 5.1 Classical end-to-end business processes in analog and digital companies

in all other areas. In the car of the future, a more-or-less simple battery and an equally simple electric motor will suffice. This will also radically change the way automotive companies think. They will no longer focus on the engine, power, torque, fuel consumption, and exhaust emissions, but on the passengers, their comfort, and safety. At the heart of the development is the software for autonomous driving. It will control everything in the car and still have enough capacity to turn the windshield into the central entertainment screen. This will be the basis for the emergence of a new entertainment industry by 2035. It will use the freed-up attention of the car-traveling public to offer them paid entertainment or provide them with diversions funded by advertising.

5.1 The Classic Company

To this day, most companies still function in a predominantly analog manner, even though they have a wide variety of digital tools at their disposal: ERP systems, email, and intranet, as well as websites or web shops. However, most processes are only partially digital, and decisions are still largely made by people—with the information for these decisions being prepared by hand, albeit with the help of Excel tools.

Traditional processes are based on a linear sequence of steps. There is a start state, and events that transform or process something to reach a state of results at the end. To this day, the sequence is still a largely people-driven process: the parts are

5.1 The Classic Company

transported from the warehouse using a forklift, a tool is retrieved from the store-room, the parts are processed and assembled with the help of machines, then packaged and prepared for shipping—and ERP software only supports these processes in full or in part. Throughout the entire process chain, there are only selective interactions between people and machines or people and software.

For decades, improvements have consisted of speeding up these processes by organizing them in a division of labor, supporting them with better and better machines, reducing idling times, increasing machine utilization, reducing errors, and so on. With tools such as Kaizen, Kanban, and Toyota 5S, these approaches are becoming more and more sophisticated, cooperation among people on the work floor is being optimized with CIP (continuous improvement processes) and with team workshops—and bonus systems are increasing people's motivation. In a further step, sensors will be used to generate and analyze data from the process so that robots can be deployed to take over individual tasks. We are currently in this phase, where robots interact with people. Only in some areas has it already been possible to fully automate one of these traditional process chains.

Until the 1980s, company headquarters employed "file schleppers" who carried folders from one office to another. They were replaced by photocopying machines, in front of which long queues of employees formed to carry individual printouts to the appropriate departments. Invoices, proposals, minutes, or reports were read in paper form, signed, forwarded, or filed away again. The procedures were thus almost exclusively performed by people, by hand. Individual attempts to improve this came with pneumatic tube mail or later with the fax, a transitional technology that half-heartedly linked the paper world with electronic data transmission. In the 1990s, data became increasingly digitized, although paper continued to be used for reading and filing. By the end of the millennium, communications were increasingly digital. As messaging now became considerably easier than walking up and down the stairs in the office, the amount of information sent back and forth increased tremendously: The "mail to all" became especially popular, with photos of puppies for sale at the company.

The increasingly used ERP systems automated parts of data transfer. Nevertheless, basically nothing had changed: the underlying linear end-to-end process still exists in most areas and is still accompanied by humans: approval processes, input processes, or revision processes. People still manually gather all the data from the system. Due to the acceleration of data transfer—instead of file schleppers and letter carriers—the pressure at the human interface increased, while the digital subsystems coped with it without any problems. Thus, since the 2000s, there were more and more stress-related symptoms of overload, up to and including complete burnout. From the 2010s onward, the pressure on people increased further, now due to constant accessibility via smartphone, with more and more people answering calls, emails, text messages, or WhatsApp messages practically around the clock. More and more companies expect their employees to be reachable even on weekends and vacations.

Due to global digitization, the amount and complexity of information to be managed has continued to increase right up until today. Since operational data processing systems only handle partial processes in an automated manner and do not make intelligent decisions, the pressure at the human interface continues to grow. The additional stress factor of "information overload" that results from this continues to burden ever wider circles of the population. Since many companies still have the same process structure today, their basic structure remains analog, and they are increasingly overwhelmed by these changes.

The only thing that will remedy this situation is artificial intelligence, which, with the help of algorithms and networked functions, will relieve humans of most everyday decisions and will be able to deal with the complexity of information in the best possible way and without errors. As a result, a large part of the workload will be taken over by machines and humans will finally be freed up to devote themselves to higher-level tasks. Why this makes sense, and not only for core processes, will be explained in the following sections on the basis of selected processes.

5.2 Interaction with the Market and Customers

In analog companies, the acquisition of new customers, the communication of the company's services, and the development of brand image are predominantly carried out by people. Information and communication campaigns are developed and implemented for this purpose. The effects of these campaigns are either not measurable at all or only in the very long term, and then it is often difficult to determine which factors are actually responsible for success or failure. If you really want to know, you have to hire a market research institute that uses a representative telephone survey with, for example, 2000 test persons to determine which commercial achieves the best results in terms of unaided brand recall. Entire departments are sent to trade fairs to represent the company or to establish contacts with customers and suppliers. Clusters and business associations organize network meetings to help relevant partners find each other. The resulting success for the companies—publicity, orders, or purchases—is based to a large extent on chance as well as on the individual talents of the people sent, on matching factors that are difficult to control and on the affinities that arise between two or more people.

In the fully digitized business, on the other hand, it is possible to carry out any desired analysis immediately. Using data on search behavior, time spent in the relevant section of the website, or click rate, precise statistics can be generated, which are subsequently used to improve performance. In addition, this data can be used to analyze exactly who the right customers are and how best to reach them. In the analog company, this information was and is still very much concentrated in the person of the sales representative. Since this tacit knowledge is also the basis for a certain position of power, it has not always been passed on to company management, which meant that considerable potential was lost.

It should also be noted that personal, person-to-person contact will continue to play an essential role, especially in B2B business and for high-value products or those requiring explanation. However, this contact will receive considerable support from data—in other words, all transaction data will be recorded and fed into the self-learning system in order to optimize the activities of these sales persons beyond their personal intuition.

A very time-consuming process in an analog company is, for example, the preparation of a bid for a tender. This can best be described using the example of a general planner in the construction industry. He or she has to break down the entire project into the sub-services and elements to be delivered and describe them precisely in terms of their scope and all of their qualitative characteristics. This results in bidding texts of over 100 pages with thousands of items, which in turn have to be priced by the bidding construction companies at the interface. The general planner estimating costs is driven to a great extent by experience and intuition. On the one hand, he or she must try to keep prices low in order to win the contract—on the other hand, he or she must calculate high enough for the contract to be profitable for the company. Ultimately, this task could be easily calculated using individual algorithms and all of the data available. However, since this is not the case in the analog company, an employee's gut feeling in combination with hundreds of small analog processes decides on the success or failure of large projects amounting to millions of euros. Moreover, this incredibly complex, time-consuming, and error-prone process has nothing to do with the actual value created by the company—namely, building the object.

In today's analog construction companies, the use of digital technologies only supports the process in certain segments. With CAD plans, quantities and dimensions no longer have to be calculated with ruler, pencil, and calculator, and tendering tools allow sample texts to be used and totals to be calculated. Nevertheless, these tools still work largely in isolation, are not networked with other functions, and require a high degree of human supervision.

In the self-supervising construction company, for example, it is sufficient to enter the digital plan with the definition of all details. Based on the current data from all areas of the company—resources, capacity utilization, empirically recorded expenditures, bidding data from the past, forecasts, seasonal and economic effects—the self-learning and thus ever-improving algorithm calculates the bid in seconds with the highest precision and transmits it in digital form. If desired, a manual check and approval can be carried out beforehand.

5.2.1 Helpdesk and Customer Hotline

Even though it seems that the help desk or support has already been highly digitized in many companies, it still functions according to the principles of the analog company and ends up annoying people rather than contributing positively to customer loyalty and customer referrals. As a first move, companies try to make reference to the FAQs on their website (the most frequently asked questions), to which standardized answers are then offered. A semi-digital variant is based on the use of chats in which service staff answer questions—or on a Teamview function in which IT service logs onto one's desktop to solve a problem. Often, people would prefer to speak to someone, but can't find the hotline on the website since it is so well hidden. If they do manage to call, the line is either busy for an eternity or they encounter a digitized voice that guides them through a problem-solving menu using numeric keys. Even if the supposed destination is finally reached after 20 minutes, it is not unusual for the caller to then be disconnected.

As these examples show, these partially digitized solutions are highly unsatisfactory from the perspective of both the company and its customers. The great potential in the self-driving company lies in the ongoing identification of its underlying problems and the equally intelligent and rapid development of improvements. Simple problems can then either be solved by customers themselves in an intuitive way, or they can receive friendly, immediate personal support on request. The self-driving company can afford this kind of support, as only a small fraction of previous support requests are still being made, and overall productivity will have been improved enormously.

5.3 Value-Adding Processes, Logistics, and Production

The value-adding processes, often called core processes, receive the most attention in the vast majority of analog companies. As a result, a higher degree of digitization has already taken place in this area than in supporting processes.

5.3.1 From the Idea to the Product

As a general rule, the value-creating process extends from the development of an idea to the finished product. To this day, new products are developed primarily on the basis of ideas created by people. Even the development of the prototype, testing on a test market or with selected customers is done almost exclusively by people and in an analog fashion. This will probably continue to be the case in the future—although considerably better data will be available to enable decisions to be made more effectively in advance on the type, content, and scope of products or services. The underlying analytics have been around for decades, but now they can be fed with much more relevant, timely, and diverse data than ever before. For example, conjoint analysis based on precise data on customer preferences, usage, and purchasing behavior can be used to create complex links with existing and desired product features that can be used as the basis for idea generation and prototype development. Based on the comprehensive and highly up-to-date data, precise forecasts of future purchasing behavior can be made even at this early stage, which in turn can be incorporated into optimization processes (Ziegler, 2019).

So while the creative process in product development is still essentially controlled by people, increasing digitization is opening up a wide range of opportunities to support product development. Netflix, for example, is already producing just one season of a series based on a creative idea and can immediately test it on the market via digital channels with the lowest possible distribution costs. If it proves successful, this can be easily measured using customer streaming and usage data: How many

5.3 Value-Adding Processes, Logistics, and Production

people have watched the series? How many stop watching and when? If the series is a hit on the market, larger budgets are approved for the further production of several seasons, and these too can be precisely monitored.

Algorithms will make it easier and better than ever to include the market in the development process. More than 80% of traditional analog companies fail to develop their business ideas or products because they do not take the needs of the market sufficiently into account during the development process (Altrichter et al., 2019). Only when the development team has spent months tinkering with the product in a self-indulgent manner does the realization come that basically no customer is willing to spend money on it. This realization is based on our own experiences from founding and investing in a wide variety of startups. The main reason for failure is and always has been the lack of coordination and alignment with the market.

5.3.2 From Forecast to Customer Delivery

The typical characteristic of an analog company is that sales and production are not digitally linked. This means that sales planning and production planning are largely separate processes. This lack of connection is based on the high degree of complexity of the activities in each of the two areas, the different levels of expertise, and the organizational separation of the people involved.

To this day, for example, the sales representative spends most of his or her time on business trips, where he or she gathers valuable information, but does not pass it on to the production department, where this important input could make a significant contribution to improving products and planning the quantities to be produced in advance. Even though there are repeated attempts to ensure better knowledge transfer here, this gets lost in everyday business, driven as it is by the urgency of its many small administrative tasks.

Thanks to their precise algorithms and comprehensive user data, highly digitized companies such as Amazon already identify and ship precisely calculated quantities of goods to regions where they are likely to be sold. This can then take place particularly quickly, much to the delight of its customers.

With full integration of all functions from the areas of sales and production, it is therefore possible to generate much more accurately calculated quantities of products that are also more precisely adapted to customer expectations. Overall, depending on the type of product or service, digitization and automation in this area is already well advanced as compared to other corporate functions—Industry 4.0 being the buzzword here. However—on the basis of full networking, with flexibly deployable, intelligent, and self-learning robot systems, individualized on-demand production, and continuous incorporation of market responses—considerable further potential can also be tapped in the area of production by 2035. Nevertheless, these potentials are not comparable with those that can be exploited in other areas of the company. To date, these have only been tapped to a limited extent, as the focus of the owners and managing directors has always been primarily on improving production while the underlying processes have been viewed in isolation and given too little attention.

In the future, all data from all areas will be continuously evaluated by the self-driving company and contribute to optimized functions throughout its organization. This will not only eliminate bottlenecks and disruptions in the production chain and reduce waiting times. With the complex interdependencies achieved, everyone will be able to adjust to everything in real time—based on precisely processed data in quantities that will far exceed those of analog companies. Processing will not be centralized, but decentralized. If we compare these data processing operations with the analog process of carrying documents back and forth and approving them, their unforeseen potential becomes particularly clear.

5.4 Interaction with Partners and Suppliers

Even though a great deal of IT is already used today in interaction with partners and suppliers, the processes are still basically carried out on an analog basis and many people are still involved among all the partners involved. Although bids, orders, and invoices are entered using Word, Excel, and the like, they are still entered manually into their respective ERP systems. At the partner's site, they are then printed out and reviewed, discussed or approved. Then, in a further step in the process, these quotations, orders, and invoices are entered into the partner's ERP system, once again by hand.

At the turn of the millennium, the vision of corporate purchasing was that it would make an active and sustainable contribution to expanding a company's competitiveness by procuring materials, products, and services with a high level of quality and service on time and on terms aligned with the market.

In our consulting projects of the last two decades, the following topics have been of strategic importance for the interaction with suppliers:

- There should be a focus on specialized departments, in order to ensure a specialized orientation and also to guarantee the satisfaction of these specialized departments.
- Intensive interaction with suppliers should act as a driver of innovation and contribute to a sensible reduction of the level of vertical integration and a concentration on strategic suppliers.
- Cost reductions should be achieved by leveraging synergies, reducing maverick buying, and using best-practice approaches from the market.
- There should be an effort to continuously optimize and automate procurement behavior and continuously professionalize the active opening of purchasing departments and procurement processes.
- The implementation of managed service models should increase the flexibility of procured materials, products, and services.
- There should be an expansion of the proactivity of strategic purchasing and the activities of specialized purchasing based on performance indicators.

One of the greatest current challenges in procurement for analog and digital companies is the conducting of large international tendering processes. A tender is a procedural model for awarding contracts competitively while adhering to the principles set out by the purchasing policy. In the context of a tender, bidders are invited to submit a written offer. Due to the competitive situation for bidders, invitations to tender ensure that bids are prepared in line with the market and offer good value for the money. In order to achieve an objectively competitive situation, several independent bidders should always be included in any given tender. In the case of invitations to tender, the relevant specialized department represents the content-related point of view, while purchasing provides the commercial perspective. Tenders represent the most important tool that purchasing departments have for obtaining the best value for the money from their suppliers.

For the future of the self-driving company, smooth interaction with a partner is only possible if the partner has the same level of automation and the appropriate interface to the company. Thus, those companies will be preferred as partners whose interface management can be largely automated. In future, for example, invitations to tender and bidding procedures between self-driving companies will be handled completely automatically. These procurement procedures can best be compared with the highly automated purchase and sale of stakes in a company by means of shares. The buyers and sellers define their negotiation parameters and the software systems handle the negotiations.

5.5 Finance and Accounting—and Corporate Management

Financial planning up to and including the reporting stage is a topic of high interest, especially for managing directors. These managers or CFOs would like nothing better than the following scenario: They plan a project with an expected profit of X millions in profit. Then all they need to do is press a button and the profit is automatically realized a year later in exactly the same way.

Especially in an analog company, countless unexpected events can occur in that subsequent year, resulting in deviations from this desired scenario: In the negative case, for example, a personnel bottleneck, delayed deliveries, a plant breakdown, a drop in demand, the entry of new competitors, or the bankruptcy of a major customer or supplier. In the positive case, an unexpected large order, a new record piece-rate in production, the surprising sale of old stock, or a drastic reduction in purchase prices due to a surplus on the world market.

The central challenge in planning has always been to recognize what the data processed are based upon. These are first of all the given facts of the company as well as forecasts for the future. For example, in order to generate a million in profits, the company would have to attract 15% new customers in this period. To do this, it would need three new employees in the sales force, the cost of which, however, would also have to be accounted for in the planning calculation.

While up until now this has mainly been done on an analog basis, supported by calculation programs, these computations can be highly automated in the future of the self-driving company. Even if not all the uncertainties of future scenarios can be eliminated, forecasts will become much more accurate due to the considerably larger data stock available in the company. For in future the current situation of the company will always be retrievable in real time—with no need to wait for the results of the tax advisor's calculations. In addition, the company will have considerably more data on its suppliers and other partners since the interfaces connecting them will be automated and all data will come in from this side in real time as well. Moreover, the systems will include Big Data analyses in their forecasts—comparable to the information prepared by Michael Bloomberg or Harvard Analytics—which many large companies already use to provide their forecasts with greater reliability.

5.5.1 From Record to Report

All processes in operational finance should have been fully automated long ago, because there is a clear set of rules that could form the basis for the corresponding programs. Nevertheless, to this day, all underlying processes are still carried out by an accounting staff that spends the whole day entering figures and data into documents and then processing them. A not inconsiderable part of their time is spent urging customers to provide receipts or data. In principle, the entire data set would be perfectly clear at all interfaces when an order is placed given the clearly ascertainable progress of the activities linked to it. Nevertheless, legions of employees still type out what others have typed in on a daily basis—even though ERP systems are now already creating many functions that could take over a significant proportion of these activities.

In the self-driving company of 2035, a demand is automatically recognized, on this basis the system places the order, and it is recorded how and when the service is provided. When the electronic invoice reaches the recipient, payment is triggered, and the service is automatically booked correctly. This does not require any documents such as an order, order confirmation, delivery confirmation, invoice, or payment confirmation. These documents are replaced by an exchange of basic data. All partial steps here are based on simple algorithms, which can be used by the system effortlessly, with maximum transparency and traceability down to the last detail. A confirmed demand triggers the complete process chain and everything runs in a highly automated manner.

It is therefore quite absurd even today how highly analog these processes still are. There are many reasons for this: clinging to what is known and proven, fear of change, need for job security, preservation of the positional power of department heads, inadequate and conservative training, and a lack of foresight on the part of management, whose horizon only extends as far as strategic 3-year goals.

Another reason is that, to this day, the mindset comes from an analog perspective rather than a digital one. This means that, according to the wishes of the managing directors, the processes should be carried out by machines in the same way as they are carried out by people—which means leaving unexploited the diverse potentials that already exist today. Instead, future potentials that in the coming years could be further advanced by artificial intelligence and deep learning are simply being ignored.

By rigidly adhering to linear process thinking, analog structures remain in place, despite the implementation of new software. The vision of this book seeks to make a significant contribution to preventing this kind of thinking. Instead of looking into the past of analog processes, there should be an attractive image of the future, in which all functions take place independently and intelligently, continuously coordinating with each other in real time and relieving humans of routines. The latter can access a complete overview of the company's overall situation at any time and, if desired, take corrective action to achieve long-term strategic goals.

Thus, people will continue to work in accounting, only they will not be forever performing the same tasks, but will have the creative freedom to make improvements and develop intelligent, completely legitimate accounting structures. In part, the proposals for these design options will come from the system and come with all the medium- and long-term effects and scenarios required. People can then discuss these options and sign off on them as needed.

5.5.2 From Strategy to Management

Up until now, the development of a strategy has been based primarily on the skills of the people who are entrusted with this task. Mostly it is experience or gut feeling, skill set and potency or power. From a theoretical perspective, there are also three factors: data, analysis, and simulation. All three of these factors can be captured and processed digitally.

To date, however, all processes are carried out by humans, albeit in part supported by reports generated with the help of an ERP system or calculation programs. In order to build on gut feeling or experience, strategy meetings are often held with department managers, sales representatives, product managers, marketing managers, and controlling. Here, the various scenarios are discussed, suggestions and objections are made, before the potency factor ultimately decides, with the CEO making his or her decision toward the end of the workshop. To a large degree, the success of the company in the next 3–5 years will depend on this decision. Consequently, operational plans are then derived from the strategy, the success of which is reviewed by middle management at shorter intervals to ensure that their goals have been achieved. The grand strategy, on the other hand, can no longer be reviewed or evaluated, as the data basis remains largely obscured by the CEO's gut feeling. Thus, something that is by and large very unclear and fuzzy is monitored and executed very rigorously to the letter, to three decimal places, on the basis of meticulously prepared subplans. In addition, the human factor comes into play once again in the implementation of the operational plans, in that power struggles are waged in the individual departments, information is blocked, or the persons seemingly responsible are replaced.

This shows that one of the most important functions in the company is governed to a large extent by emotions and intuition rather than by systematically working through strategies on the basis of secure data and then making a decision that is fully comprehensible in all its individual aspects. In the self-driving company of 2035, far more data will underlie these decisions than do today, and all of it is recorded in the system and can be evaluated in every conceivable way. All scenarios developed in this way can be presented along with all the effects they will have on the company as a whole. This means that a secure database is already available at the time of the strategic decision, from which operational plans are automatically generated. There is no longer any need for intervals at which interim reports are submitted; instead, any deviation from the set targets is recorded in real time in every area of the overall system. On this basis, a report is sent to management, if desired, on the basis of a predefined level of deviation; it is linked to various options for correcting these results, including all associated prognoses for all areas of the company. Whereas in the past it often took years to receive feedback for specific actions, this now occurs more on an ongoing basis in real time. This significantly increases the level of certainty and reduces the level of risk in the company.

The people actively involved in the process have a completely transparent basis for making decisions on an ongoing basis that can be reconstructed down to the smallest detail. What's more, you can use this data to develop ideas that reach beyond the system's radius of action—such as for creative new products that could be developed on the basis of horizontal or vertical diversification, or for opening up new markets in new countries or a niche that has opened up due to current social or technological developments.

In this regard, the analogous strategy can be compared to a big old oil tanker that finds its way on the basis of the captain's experience, grasps dangers much too late, and reacts only sluggishly to the maneuvers of the helmsman. The new strategy can be compared to a swarm of small, extremely fast boats that constantly communicate with each other and synchronize their information from hundreds of perspectives, always striving to move forward as safely and quickly as possible. If unexpected problems occur, only a few boats will be affected, and they will immediately communicate their situation to everyone, leading to immediate corrections by all the other boats.

Because in such a decentralized system the decisions to be made continuously do not come in a rigid hierarchical manner from above, but are made continuously by all actors in mutual coordination on the basis of a higher-level strategy, there are also no idle times caused by a lack of decisions or by insufficient communication of the decisions from the top down. The many small decisions concerning a network always find their way to their target. In addition, the secure and transparent data basis allows the staff to better understand and thus accept all decisions and actions taken. This releases enormous potential for improving the performance of the entire company.

Another aspect is the "fail fast" principle, which has a long tradition in the USA and is now increasingly being used in Europe as well: you are welcome to try something, but you should quickly recognize if it does not work. This principle is not

5.5 Finance and Accounting—and Corporate Management

yet practiced by analog companies in the same way, whereas the digital enterprise opens up far-reaching opportunities for this. These opportunities also ensure that it is initially much easier and quicker to determine and communicate exact forecast models on the basis of a given idea. This also makes it much easier to calculate opportunities and risks and to test the implementation of the idea, for example in the form of a field trial on a test market. Without having to hire an expensive market research institute, all customer reactions to the new product are recorded and evaluated. This approach will be standard in 2035, especially because it has long been the practice of digital companies—as exemplified by Internet start-ups in 2020. For instance, new products are posted in web stores and all customer reactions are immediately recorded: How many people click on the product? How long do they stay on the page? How do they move around the page? Which types of customers buy the product? Already today, a variety of data is captured in real time and can be analyzed immediately. Subsequently, it can be checked whether the product should remain on the market or not. Or the existing product range can be used to build up a new market by launching the web store in Brazil, for example. Here, too, solid and diverse data will be available in a short time, which will form the basis for just such management decisions—and this, for example, for the entire Brazilian market.

With the fully digitized company, it will thus be possible to control complexity to a far greater extent. Until today, it was precisely this complexity that made it necessary in autonomous companies to work with the unreliable instrument of gut feeling. This intuition represents the accumulation of people's lifelong experiences and processes them according to incomprehensible algorithms. This is by no means to say that this gut feeling is entirely bad. Many studies in behavioral economics show that decisions made on the basis of gut feeling are systematically better than those based on hard information.

Today, the "hard facts" available in analog companies are not only inadequate, but in the increasingly complex environment, far from sufficient to be used as the basis for sound strategic decisions. Even in the future of the self-driving company, not all information will be available—but the proportion will be far higher, so that the quality and quantity of the data, together with the diverse algorithms, will provide a better basis for decision-making than ever before.

The complexity problem will thus be handled to a large extent by machines, making it much easier for the managers concerned to think. They no longer have to strain their intuition by using it to check the quality of strategic scenarios. Instead, they will be freed from these burdens and will be able to broaden their perspective and increase the distance their view takes in. They will be challenged to think beyond the existing and by now well-functioning strategic, tactical, and operational system. Any ideas based on these insights will be discussed within the teams and, if they are considered to be good, implemented on a trial basis. If the idea does not work, it can be quickly abandoned.

5.6 Organization and Personnel

Many organizations face the challenge of responding to changes in the market, new technologies, growing competition from start-ups, customer demands, and a lack of human resources. Companies are thus constantly exposed to internal and external influences and/or changes. In classic organizational forms, specialized departments often cannot keep up with the speed of these changes, given the way they work, leaving them unable to use the human potential that is actually available.

5.6.1 From Personnel Planning to Recruiting

Recruiting new personnel is a lengthy process that starts with the identification of positions. For these positions, a wide range of information must be collected in the company and compiled in the personnel office. This includes medium- and long-term forecasts for the company's success, capacities to be built up or cut back in production or administration, as well as other figures and data on the company's performance and efficiency. In addition, there are personal wishes and vanities. There are always managers who manage to gather a particularly large number of assistants around them and others who are more frugal and achieve the same output with fewer resources. There are managers who whine more loudly than others that they can't get by with their present staff and others who are perhaps better organized and who manage to achieve their goals even with fewer resources. Ultimately, therefore, the creation of staff positions is a mix of hard and soft facts as well as irrational, emotional aspects—even if the people involved are often not aware of this.

In large companies, an additional position is calculated as requiring approximately one million euros in capital. These are the internal costs for employing someone full-time over several decades. These consist of the combined wage costs, taxes, and required equipment, such as a desk, car, or computer.

The first consideration in determining staffing needs is to try to fill the gap through internal redeployment. If this does not work, a position is created, and then the move is made to the personnel market. Initially, this is usually done unofficially by searching for suitable candidates within personal networks. If this search remains unsuccessful, the personnel market is involved. For this purpose, a job profile is generated with all the requirements and incentives of the position, and the personnel advertisement is placed or posted in the relevant online and offline media, such as on the company website, in job portals, regional or national newspapers, social media such as LinkedIn and Xing and, in the case of the search for apprentices and skilled workers, also by means of a notice board on company premises.

This starts the next, lengthy stage of the process, with online and offline applications coming into the company. Depending on the quantity of applicants, knockout criteria are first applied to reduce the number of applications. These knockout criteria may well be cynical, racist, or misogynistic and ensure that the portrait photo is already reason enough for excluding an application. However, since

5.6 Organization and Personnel

these criteria are applied unofficially and only a small circle of people is privy to them, it is ensured that the criteria are not communicated to the outside in the sense of attractive "employer branding."

The next stage of the process involves making personal contact, arranging meetings, and further screening of applicants. For higher-paying jobs, personnel agencies or headhunters are called in or internal assessment centers are conducted.

In the self-driving company of 2035, positions are defined on the basis of comprehensive internal and external information that is continuously processed by a wide range of algorithms. The system knows about the current and long-term workload in the company, creates reliable forecasts and scenarios, calculates the monetary and operational consequences of a new appointment, and suggests a further course of action based on a job profile.

The way in which the application process of the future will differ from analog processes can already be guessed at today on the basis of common practice in China. There, in larger companies—once use has been made of personal networks, which continue to be relevant there too—applications are predominantly made via social media. Instead of the lengthy process of writing letters of application, applicants only need to press a button to send their data to the company. There, this information can be processed immediately, and an automated matching process takes place based on the desired applicant profile, resulting in the desired number of best applicants. Only then is contact established and the applicants are personally assessed in more detail.

5.6.2 From Investment to Divestment

In an analog company, the entire resource management is based on highly manual processes. All acquisitions and investments are based on decisions made by employees in the appropriate areas, which are approved personally or with the involvement of the next higher level, depending on the size of the investment.

Analog companies are still far from imagining that these processes could be digitized, and the potential to be leveraged by doing so is unknown. Companies believe they are already in a position to operate in a highly modernized manner just because parts of the core processes, such as in production, have already been automated. While minor productivity increases are achieved in production with ERP systems, there is enormous untapped potential in resource management. Instead of linear end-to-end processes, networked entrepreneurial algorithms could be used here as well. Here, too, humans would only have to intervene to support decisions that lie outside the defined system framework.

This is best illustrated by an example: In the networked overall system of the self-driving company of 2035, it is reported that a new machine is needed because a market that has just been tapped for a product variant has resulted in a 3% increase in capacity utilization. Based on the company's internal data, which has been continuously collected in production for years, the specifications for the machine are clearly defined: An intelligent agent system is used to compare the requirements for throughput, maintenance and maintenance intensity, energy demand, quality of output, flexibility, and maneuverability with the machines offered on the world market and, in this way, the best bidders are determined. If desired, the list of results can then be viewed by the appropriate purchasing representative and further negotiation will take place on a person-to-person basis. Smaller routine procurements are fully automated up to and including payment and the correct taxation of the invoice.

For new or more complex issues, a self-organizing team (see Sect. 6.5.1) is used, a kind of "bubble" that is supplied with all the information prepared by the system and can then solve the task collaboratively with high efficiency. For example, the data for a work process that has not yet been digitized can be determined with a Digital Twin. This data is in turn fed into the overall system and new alternative solutions are calculated by the algorithms. Similar bubbles also exist in other areas of the company; all teams are continuously supplied with the latest information by the network of intelligent software. Thus, there is no rigid top-down hierarchy, but largely autonomous teams that achieve high-quality results based on up-to-date information aligned with the overall optimum of the system. All results, in turn, improve the performance of the company and, in the spirit of complete transparency, can be viewed at any time, if required, and with regard to all associated decision-making criteria.

In order to create incentives within this system for the people involved, a wide range of possibilities are available. For example, a large variety of bonus systems can be tested and analyzed in terms of their positive effects, how far they contribute to improving the achievement of strategic goals or to increasing marginal returns. These and other easily applicable levers will make it much easier for management to handle complexity in the future.

5.6.3 Facility Management

The goal of good facility management is to manage one or more buildings or properties in such a way that the lowest possible costs are incurred. Due to the complexity and high savings potential of this undertaking, facility management has also established itself as a science in its own right. Up to now, the information to be processed has always been recorded and combined in analog form, as from the following areas:

- Procurement
- Utilization, leasing
- Sales
- Heating, ventilation, sanitation
- Building automation
- Staff organization
- IT infrastructure
- Vehicle fleet
- Maintenance, servicing
- Cleaning

There are therefore many interfaces within and outside the company, with strategic management, department heads, building services, staff representatives, tenants, and the various service providers. These are all managed in terms of the classic processes, with a lot of communication work required to obtain an optimized solution in each case, for example, in the design and distribution of office workstations, the commissioning of an electricity supplier, or the maintenance of the heating system. As can be concluded from the findings so far, many facility management functions can be automated and networked with each other in the future. One system continuously searches for the best or, in terms of sustainability goals, cleanest electricity provider and switches automatically, thus supplying the fleet of e-cars and e-bikes with the cheapest electricity at any given time of day. Another subsystem tracks the activities of the employees and draws conclusions for the optimized arrangement of the workstations, while the entire building automation system ensures an ideal indoor climate in a coordinated manner by means of heating, ventilation, cooling, sun protection, and core activation of the wall surfaces.

References

Altrichter, M., Ertler, M., Fassl, L.-M., et al. (2019). *Startup investing: Praxishandbuch für Investorinnen und Investoren*. Linde.

Ziegler, M. (2019). Marktforschung. In N. Baur & J. Blasius (Eds.), *Handbuch Methoden der empirischen Sozialforschung* (2nd ed., pp. 191–202). Springer VS.

The Self-Driving Company

6

For about 15–20 years now, all the technologies have been available to completely automate production, to create a "glass factory." All major consulting firms have repeatedly shown that this is theoretically as well as practically possible. However, only a few companies have implemented it so far. The Tesla, for example, could already roll off the assembly line today—assuming it was produced in a single version—in a completely automated manner. By adding a little more software intelligence, the production of variants would also be possible. The reason why this has not been implemented to date is the cost of robots and that it has been cheaper to manufacture with a combination of human labor and automation. Nevertheless, disproportionately more has been invested in the technologization and digitization of the value-adding processes than in the accompanying business processes. In the coming years, companies will invest in digitization, automation, and learning software systems specifically in these accompanying business processes.

In the next five sections, the future corporate areas of market and customers, interaction with suppliers and partners, value creation, finance, and organization will be described along with the changes they will undergo. The new roles and tasks of customers, partners, owners, and staff will be explored. Self-driving organizations do not have classic end-to-end processes, but algorithms make decisions continuously based on data. This transformation is described and the resulting organizational form explained.

6.1 Interaction with Market and Customers

In the technologization and automation of recent years, the interface to customers has often been neglected. This has also been shown by our internal company studies. There has been a lot of research and development, but ultimately nothing has been invested in this area. Some developments even went in the wrong direction. Digital trade shows represent an example of this: here potential technical possibilities were

© The Author(s), under exclusive license to Springer-Verlag GmbH, DE, part of Springer Nature 2023
F. Schnitzhofer, *The Self-Driving Company*, Future of Business and Finance, https://doi.org/10.1007/978-3-662-68148-0_6

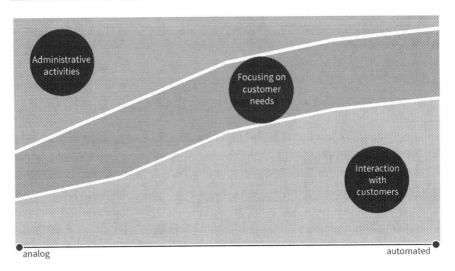

Fig. 6.1 Improving interaction with customers through automation (Real example)

far from being exploited. In fact, digital trade shows only reproduce the analog world in digital form, with virtual 3D trade show booths and avatars that move back and forth on the artificial trade show floor. Sure, there are advantages here, the trade fair can be reached without travel expenses and is available 24/7 all over the world. Ultimately, though, there are only a few technocrats who are enthusiastic about this solution, and digital trade fairs continue to plod along without achieving any decisive breakthrough.

The goal of good sales is clearly defined: to sell new customers one's own products, to sell existing customers additional products or services, or to sell the latter existing products at higher prices. It can therefore be assumed that the topics of sales and marketing will gain considerably in importance over the next 5 years. Compared to the production processes, which algorithms are already good at controlling, the interaction with the customer is the most complex challenge of digitization. At the same time, a marketing-oriented company must base all of its functions on customer demand. This means that interaction with customers triggers all other operational functions (see Fig. 6.1).

For sales personnel, the use of these algorithms means a fundamental improvement in their work situation, since they previously had to spend a large proportion of their daily working time on administrative activities and ultimately had less time available to attend directly to the personal needs of customers and to their personal relationships with them. The self-driving company thus gives sales staff back their valuable time for personal relationship management with potential customers.

For thousands of years, the trade of goods and services has been based on the sales skills of those directly involved in this trade. The basic principles of successful sales have not changed, even in the age of digitization. The most important stages in winning a customer have always remained the same: The company must draw

6.1 Interaction with Market and Customers

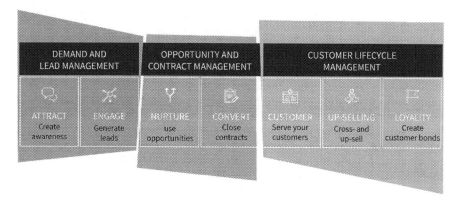

Fig. 6.2 Focus topics for interaction with customers

attention to its product and arouse the customer's interest. Now the golden ingredient of sales is added to our recipe: potential customers must have an existing or at least latent need for the product, or the salesperson must be able to convince them of the need. Once interest has been aroused, the sales opportunity must be developed and ultimately brought to a conclusion. This involves the contractual and pricing arrangements and the mutual commercial convergence of supply and demand. Only the concluded sales contract or the signed offer is considered an actual sales success. Many would assume that sales ends at this point. However, this is one of the biggest misconceptions. Especially the subsequent actions in the sales process bring strong sales and margins in the long run. The goal is to turn existing customers into loyal customers and ultimately into fans and ambassadors of the products. This is achieved through intensive customer care, even after the product has been purchased. The focus in the customer life cycle is on cross-selling and upselling. Selling existing customers additional services or, if applicable, additional products is the supreme challenge in sales. The "icing on the sales cake" is the transformation of one-time or repeat customers into brand ambassadors. Based on their recommendation of our product to other customers, they then take over sales and marketing for the companies.

Figure 6.2 shows the three areas in which customer interaction will be shaped in the future:

1. First, the need must be awakened.
2. Then, the potential customers must be turned into actual customers. The requirements for opportunity and contract management increase with the complexity of the products and their need for explanation.
3. Customer life cycle management begins once the contract has been formed.

Much of the company's profit margin lies in customer life cycle management. This can best be illustrated by the example of buying a car. Dealers generate the relevant margins not at the time of purchase, but during the further life cycle of the vehicle by means of upselling through service and repair activities or via spare parts. At the same time, in this phase three, good companies try to turn customers into real fans who then act as brand ambassadors and convince their acquaintances of the value of the company's products.

6.1.1 Growth Hacking Instead of Marketing

The cultivation of new markets or customers has undergone a massive change in recent years. Domains such as classic marketing have been replaced by modern data-driven methods such as "growth hacking." This is a set of methods taken from the start-up scene. Classic marketing techniques are enhanced using creativity, digital sales approaches, analytical evaluation methods, and new digital platforms. The evaluation of data and trends plays a very important role. In addition, software solutions are used to open up new channels to potential customers. The goal of growth hacking is for customers to become aware of the company's own products on their own, to recognize their own needs, and to buy the product on their own. An important element in the digital approach to potential customers is the omni-channel user experience. Communication and the customer experience must be available in the same way across all digital *and* analog channels. In the digitized present and future, it is not the sales department that chooses the sales channel; quite the opposite, this department responds to the needs of the customers. Here, the focus is on customer demand and customer accessibility. Even if this means using a Chinese chat provider in sales. Website content must communicate the same brand message as print media, email marketing, and social media content do. Personalized customer advice and product purchase should be possible via each and every channel (cf. Fig. 6.3).

In the course of digitization, far more customer data will be available to show companies exactly how these people interact with their products and services, what behavior patterns they exhibit, or what habits they have. In addition, companies will also know what their customers do otherwise, what media they consume, for example, and what their areas of interest are. This data is relevant for communications work, for awakening new customer demand. All of the data flows into further product development, whereby the primary aim is not only to further develop *existing* products. Here, people are again called upon to make use of their creativity and all of their findings to create completely new and disruptive solutions.

Market communication is becoming much more precisely targeted. Whereas up to now, especially in the B2C sector, advertising spots about furniture, for example, have generated considerable scatter loss, future digital possibilities will reduce this. In the future, furniture retailers will communicate precisely with those people who actually have a need because they are in the midst of furnishing their new house. So there is no longer a target group in the traditional sense, no longer any rough clusters that are then narrowed down. The relevant sales contacts are determined dynamically from the ongoing data. At the moment, Amazon has already made headway along this path. In the future, a personality profile will be created for every single customer

6.1 Interaction with Market and Customers

Fig. 6.3 Illustration of the interdisciplinarity of growth hacking

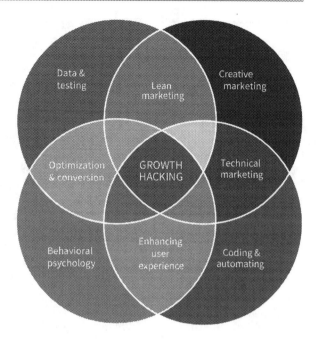

with regard to all the parameters and data recorded. The entire communication and later the products as well will be based on this profile and tailored to the individual.

The mantra is: Know your customer! Amazon and Facebook already know all their customers, but most companies are still a long way from this. At the most, the sales team knows one or the other major customer inside out with regard to his or her needs. Time and again, it becomes apparent that they do not pass this information on to management and their colleagues in an adequate manner. In self-driving companies, both the process of data collection and the transmission of information are fully automated. All other operational functions are aligned with these findings. If desired, management can pull every conceivable market and sales report from the system to provide a basis for strategic decision-making. Every person appreciates it when their needs are truly addressed down to the last detail. As a result, they will also agree to allow their data to be used because they have experienced significant benefits from doing so. Accordingly companies must:

1. Create demand among the right people.
2. Tailor their products and services precisely to these people.
3. Reward loyal customers and turn them into brand ambassadors. Because in the future too, satisfied customers and their recommendations will continue to be the best means of advertising. This no longer takes place only in the form of word-of-mouth recommendations, but increasingly effectively via online platforms and social media.

Only those who perform these three functions professionally will be able to survive on the market in the future, as current developments also show. Those who have understood this for a while now are the fastest growing companies today and are miles ahead of the competition. The others are only hesitantly beginning to move in the same direction. Those that implement this professionally will profit very quickly from it. The others will be left behind in the iron age, where a pile of steel is produced and only then is a thought given to whom they could sell it. In addition, a central paradigm of growth hacking is: My products have to do marketing. As such, companies build their products to do marketing on their own behalf. The Austrian start-up Runtastic has demonstrated this particularly successfully. Once the athlete has tracked his or her run or bike tour, the data can be automatically uploaded to social media and shared. Here they are seen by a large number of friends, who in turn also become interested in purchasing the app in order to do their own runs or tours and compare themselves with their friends and other interested parties.

Growth hacking data also drives in-person sales, especially in the B2B space. As shown in the GRANOBIZ example, they have all the data relevant to their key accounts. With this valuable information, they in turn make an invaluable contribution to the business activities of their customers and thus lay a foundation for long-term planning and the development of new business areas.

In the future, however, there will also be people in the B2C sector who will be able to make use of the self-driving company's data for the benefit of their customers. Financial products that require explanation will continue to be sold from person to person. Highly individualized offers can be developed based on detailed information about the customer's complex needs. The face-to-face conversation can be supported by individualized animated videos, which can be used to play out all future scenarios.

6.1.2 Example: The Analog and Digital Furniture Retailer

An example from the field of international furniture retailing shows how an analog business model can and must be completely re-imagined. Initially, the retailer consisted of a few stores each run by a store manager. In the next step—around 2010—the retailer went online with a "digital store." This was set up professionally based of the technologies available at the time. Within a few years, it quickly developed into by far the largest store. Initially, the online store was run like a regional branch. Only in a further evolutionary step did the entire spectrum of possibilities open up: at this point the online store was no longer conceived of from the perspective of the analog market, but from the perspective of the digital world. First of all, the online store was accessible 24/7 from all over the world. In contrast to the brick-and-mortar store, it always had all of its products available, which could be called up in a flash according to a wide range of search parameters and examined with regard to all purchase-relevant parameters. Once a customer profile has been created, orders can be placed immediately, and it is possible to track

6.1 Interaction with Market and Customers

the shipping status of the product until it is delivered to the customer's home or to pick up these products directly in the physical store via "click and collect."

This explains the rapid success of the online store, while the physical stores are still largely based on a principle dating from the post-war era. At the latter, after a long journey and search in the store, an available salesperson must first be found. If it is possible to find a sofa in stock that meets one's wishes, it can only be viewed on site but not taken away. Accordingly, the process shifts awkwardly into the partially digitized world. Because the sofa is of course only physically present in the showroom. Availability is now checked on a PC in an uncomfortable alcove of the store using an outdated database. Then order forms are printed out, which have to be filled in by hand and signed several times, before the entire data set is again entered by hand to trigger the ordering process. This then takes even longer than in the "real" digital store. In addition, delivery or pickup cannot be tracked digitally. The seller only gives a rough time window for delivery, or the delivery costs are unexpectedly high. This means that the sofa has to be picked up, after all, physically on site. To find out the exact pickup date, the customer has to call again and again, only to be told—after a long wait in the queue and after entering digits as instructed by a computer voice—that the salesman is unfortunately on sick leave at the moment and the colleague doesn't know the date.

So the future will be different: the classic retail stores will not survive the competition from Amazon and Co. While Amazon shows in a radical way how the digital store works, the analog store of the near future will only survive if it represents a real counterpoint to the online world, with everything that characterizes a physical, visual, olfactory and, if possible, gustatory experience. The real on-site store will be a space of pleasure and sensuality.

The retail store of the future will resemble a cozy apartment more than a store, and it will be almost always open. The sample sofa will be available for test sitting, and the products offered there will be accompanied by easy-to-use automated tools that allow the fabric or material samples to be felt and physically experienced. The shopping experience will once again become increasingly haptic. For example, buying a complex sofa set will be more reminiscent of a Lego game. Together with an on-site consultant, the desired sofa landscape is assembled from individual small sofa modules. The digital information is processed in the background and sent to the supplier as soon as the order is placed. The customer pays digitally and takes the small sofa model home with him or her directly after the purchase. A few days later, the sofa is delivered to the customer's home, if desired with an assembler who is automatically guided by the system during assembly.

One application that is likely to be used to a greater extent again in the course of these developments is augmented reality. It involves merging the virtual world with the real world, as the Swedish retailer Ikea has already very effectively shown. However, a smartphone as a playback device is not ideal for this. Data glasses, for example, are a much better fit here. First, the new sofa model is configured and the right fabric is selected, then the data glasses are briefly put on and a photo of the existing living room is uploaded. Now the customer can look at the 3D animation of the sofa in the real situation and decide whether he or she might want to change anything else about the fabric or the configuration. This technology has been promised to us as consumers on a regular basis for the last 5–10 years. The reason we are not there yet is because of the exponential development and proliferation of technology. It will take at least until 2025 and more likely until 2030 before data glasses and augmented reality are part of our everyday lives.

6.1.3 Example: Supermarket Scenarios

The supermarket provides another example of the radical change in the way we interact with customers. It will no longer be necessary to take a shopping basket or shopping cart. We will be in the midst of pleasurable scenarios where show chefs can be observed, tastings are offered, and the associated products are simply added to one's wish list. So we walk around—much like at the classic marketplace loved for millennia—meeting friends, drinking coffee or perhaps a glass of prosecco, exchanging thoughts with each other and with the highly motivated staff about the delicacies that are on offer.

In contrast, the supermarket remains to this day a boring high-shelf warehouse, as it was created in the early twentieth century in the course of the Industrial Revolution. We have been walking around here for decades in a confusing, narrow labyrinth, desperately searching for the eggs hidden in the farthest corner of the lowest shelf. The strongest and most lasting memory in this supermarket consists of collisions with other shopping carts, bags of flour falling off shelves and bursting open, and milk cartons leaking. Then we have to wait in line at the checkout for ten minutes, watch as 1-, 2- and 5-cent coins are endlessly counted out in front of us, put everything on the conveyor belt, then back into the shopping cart, then into shopping bags, at home into the refrigerator, and only then do the goods finally make it to the table. Thus, we have to move each piece of cheese seven times from the high-shelf warehouse until it makes it onto a piece of bread.

In the sensuous market of the near future, we will only have to express our wishes—and there are many technical options here for completely individualizing the service—and then the goods will be delivered to our homes. By the way, this will also create new jobs, because we will not only be highly qualified academics and artists in the future. It is left to the imagination of each individual to decide which is more pleasant: Looking after shelves in a cramped high-shelf warehouse while being cut off from daylight, sitting at the checkout for hours under pressure—or riding around outside on an e-bike and delivering baskets of goods.

We all have cherished habits, preferring Italian prosciutto, hay milk, and finely ground whole grain rye bread. If we want to, we can integrate these things into our shopping in an automated way and not have to walk the same round in the winding supermarket over and over again. By the way, why do we do this? Because we humans love habits. That is, we love having certain things always in stock at home and experiencing the same familiar routines over and over again. What we love less is the circuit through the high-shelf warehouse. At the same time, this reveals a paradox: we were familiar with the search for our favorite groceries, navigating the

6.1 Interaction with Market and Customers

supermarket without having to work our way through the assortment of over 10,000 products. Nothing worse could happen than that the store was rearranged and the search had to start all over again. However, we did happen to find one or two interesting new products, which we then tried out. The sensory market of the future will relieve us of the burden of searching for the familiar and also confront us if we wish with interesting new things. The sellers will not be sweaty workers, but competent and empathetic moderators who will understand our wishes and develop interesting solutions together with us. We will socialize, eat a fresh lunch menu, and when we leave the store relaxed, our shopping basket will be automatically billed and delivered.

A small digression in this context, aimed primarily at manufacturers and retailers: Countless studies prove that people always buy the same detergent, throughout their lives. For decades, manufacturers have been trying with elaborate advertising campaigns to get people to wash their laundry even whiter with their detergent, but without much success. We all fiercely hold on to our favorite detergent.

In the new sensuous market of the future, it will be possible for the manufacturer to finally have a real, because personal, discussion with customers. Not a classic sales talk, but an interactive dialog in which customers talk about their habits and realize that they haven't had the right detergent for years and have finally found what they really wanted all along. This example also shows that the employee profile in retail is being considerably upgraded. These people will let us taste the new *Junghopfen* beer, accompanied by a piece of senna cheese, aged for 6 months. We may not immediately buy everything we're served here, but we'll feel comfortable, sure to come back soon—even if it's just for our standard, cherished basket of goods.

This sensuous market thus elegantly skips a stage that major suppliers like Walmart are currently feverishly working on. Here, they are experimenting with RFID chips (radio frequency identification chips) that are attached to the merchandise to track it. Cameras are installed to read when a product needs to be replenished to the high-shelf warehouse, while still maintaining shelves by hand. However, retail employees are relieved because the expiration date of the goods no longer has to be checked by hand. The check is carried out by the system, which then sends a message or ensures that the old goods are brought to the front of the shelf shortly before their expiration date—which means it's not yet a truly intelligent system. A basically banal process is partially automated and no real improvement is achieved for either customers or sales as a result. The goal for 2035 is therefore not the partially digitized high-shelf warehouse, but the stationary, sensuous, human on-site variant of the fully automated, intelligent online store that knows its customers, approaches them individually, offers a wide range of personal services, and gives sales staff the opportunity to develop their personal potential.

A transitional example of this brick-and-mortar online store is the Apple Store— here with the variant of the warehouse in the next room. In this case, in an almost completely empty designer store, we find a few highly polished devices in spacious surroundings, which are not to be moved. A hipster shows us the software on the Mac, which we then basically buy online—no shelves with boxes of packed devices. Then the colleague fetches the desired device from the warehouse and we can take our new Macbook home right away, where it will show us how to operate it in a highly automated and self-explanatory way.

Another example of brick-and-mortar online retailing—here largely digitized—are the small ATM branches of banks. In the version without any staff at all, there are only ATMs in the reception area that are available 24 h a day, 7 days a week. Access is gained by means of an ATM or credit card. As long as cash is still in circulation, these ATM branches will remain as popular as they are now. Currently, the use of these machines is the most common reason for visiting a bank branch.

But back to the "gastro experience" market of 2035: From a technical perspective, there will be a generously designed gastro showroom without any shelves. It will contain small quantities of a wide variety of products in stock, allowing shoppers to examine them at their leisure and then have them delivered. This will move the former high-shelf warehouse from expensive locations in city centers to logistically optimized locations. Opening hours will also be possible 24/7, just as in "real" online retailing since the showroom legally belongs to the gastronomy sector, and the actual retail business with goods takes place exclusively online.

With regard to delivery, further variants also make sense, completely according to customer desire. In addition to delivery directly to the customer's home, there could also be a storage box in front of the store or at another location of the customer's choice, where the shopping cart can be placed and picked up. In 2035, delivery will probably not yet be carried out exclusively by drone, but the delivery staff will be part of software-controlled teams (see also Sect. 2.4, something which is already being practiced presently. Staff members receive orders on their data glasses, together with all relevant instructions: What should be delivered where by when? How do I get there? These things already work very well using smartphone apps and will be further refined, with intuitive user interfaces that even untrained employees can quickly grasp. The overall system always knows who is where and continuously optimizes logistical processes—like a top waitress who always takes some information, an empty plate, or the soup from the kitchen with her on every trip, saving herself many miles of legwork every day compared to her less attentive colleagues.

What the basic conditions are for these delivery workers must be negotiated at a high ethical level, and this is where politics is also called upon. In any case, as has been noted for decades, there are always enough people who like to do just this kind of work, young people, students, in some cases those who have dropped out of office jobs, bike freaks who like to ride around all day, stay fit, and keep their minds free to enjoy the day, make plans for the future, or stay mentally fresh in order to take part in an online seminar in the evening. Preference is given to employers who don't put unnecessary pressure on you and where it's perfectly OK to take a break and go for a cappuccino. It's not a job you do your whole life—but it's definitely fun for a while. Besides, the job at the Federal Railroad from apprenticeship to early retirement at 55 is already a thing of the past anyway.

6.1.4 The Future Shape of Retailing

While the supermarket example showed how retail is evolving into brick-and-mortar online retail, there will also be other variants in the sense of the self-driving company. Taking GRANOBIZ as an example, here the company will in part supply retailers, but a significant portion of its sales will go directly to regular customers or end consumers. These customers are real fans who become brand ambassadors by enthusiastically talking about their individualized sports bar during the racing bike tour in the group: a bar that is tailored precisely to their needs for micronutrients, secondary plant substances with a balanced ratio of easily digestible, vegan proteins, omega-3 fatty acids, and slow-release carbohydrates.

This direct sales approach has a history of decades of proven success, as exemplified by Tupperware, which has been an international hit since 1938 and continues to be one today. Sales take place without intermediaries and a sustainable, close relationship is built up with the end consumers, ensuring self-perpetuating dissemination and referrals, and ongoing new customers. An interesting current aspect—ever since Tupper tried to set up an online store, the company has run into difficulties, as this strategy undermines its own recipe for success. In other words, the opportunities offered by digitization have not been properly exploited. A blanket statement should not be made about what the right form of retailing looks like; it must always be decided individually from manufacturer to manufacturer and from retailer to retailer. In 2035, it will still be the needs of the customers that will determine which variant is the best. In many cases, it will be based on the omni-channel principle, with direct sales to clientele, flagship stores for brand manufacturers, and retailers who continue to carry several brands in their product line and create a diverse shopping experience.

In the case of products that require explanation, it is also conceivable that appointments for personal meetings could be made online. Either the experts would come to the customer's home or office on request—or they would meet in a brick-and-mortar branch to discuss the details of these larger deals. Based on a high degree of digitization, this branch could also be used flexibly, for instance, by several providers. Here, samples could either be visualized on site, via 3D, for example, or haptic parts could also be taken away physically—up to and including products as large and complex as an automobile. This is shown by the example of Tesla, which the end customer has long been able to order and configure in a strictly online way. But people want the showroom here, want to smell the leather, feel the acceleration of the test car, and put together their e-car in cooperation with a personal contact person who responds to questions and wishes competently and individually.

In 2035, the "gastro experience" market will also carry a more diverse range of products, as there will no longer be any need to maintain an established, physical order in the high-shelf warehouse. Every product will be instantly accessible upon request. It is conceivable, for example, that the supplier will enter into a new and agile relationship with the retailer by agreeing on a specific display area with or without personal support, on which conditions will then be based. Customers already have the standard products in their shopping carts anyway, so more attention will be paid to what is new and special, making it easier for new suppliers to enter the market. This may include small, regional suppliers, organic farmers who can sell their products at the local "gastro experience" market and at the same time benefit from the online presence of the large retail chains.

With automation, the physical structure of businesses is also changing. I remember standing in the reception area of a large Austrian bank and watching an angry customer trying to complain to the corresponding online direct bank, whose parent organization is this traditional Austrian bank. Of course, he could not be sent to the corresponding department, because it consisted only of a handful of programmers who maintain the website and system. The direct bank did not provide the opportunity to meet personally with a supervisor. However, this allowed the products to be offered at lower prices. It will take a few more years for consumers to get used to the two service variants. There will be the high-priced service offerings and the low-priced online-only offerings. Both variants have their justification on the market. However, people need to learn about the advantages and also the disadvantages of both offerings. Price is increasingly being pushed into the background as service and quality gain priority in the perception of value.

6.2 Interaction with Partners and Suppliers

The relationship with partners and suppliers in the self-driving organization is significantly driven by the extent to which that organization is self-driving. Initially, we assume that all selected partners also have this status. Tenders for series material are then completely automated via e-procurement platforms. These systems intelligently decide on the material to be procured and the ideal manufacturer or supplier.

The human contribution in the interaction with partners and suppliers lies primarily in establishing the initial contact and building a personal relationship, as well as in negotiating the framework conditions for the cooperative venture. Subsequently, the self-driving company takes over the handling of all agendas within the framework agreement based on the requirements as they arise. This also means that in the future there will always be people working in sales as well as in purchasing with personal commitment, expertise, charisma, and empathy. There and with larger individual procurements such as industrial machinery, there will therefore continue to be "a human side." For mass-produced goods such as screws and commodities, on the other hand, purchasing will be completely automated. Here, due to the possibilities of global sourcing, diverse offers will be continuously registered and evaluated by digital, adaptive agents in order to make the best decision for the company.

Procurement is thus tracked digitally, just as the sales process described above is. At the time of procurement, all related activities are already fully automated in real time, from storage space to production capacity—and in the case of further processing of a capital good, all the way to the delivery date to the customer. The order is assigned a QR code, for example, with which the goods are tagged and with which they can subsequently be tracked on their way through the company. Humans

6.2 Interaction with Partners and Suppliers

will hardly be required here, if at all, right up to issuing the invoice. The latter will also be generated and approved fully automatically, as the software used, which is networked with all operational functions, will have all the information about the quality and scope of the service provided by the suppliers at its disposal on an ongoing basis.

Invoices having to be checked, signed, and approved by several people will have become a thing of the distant past. After all, when an order is placed, the customer basically accepts that an invoice will have to be paid if the delivery is correct, regardless of whether it involves the delivery of 10,000 tons of steel or the painting contractor repainting the office. As a result of the fully digital and error-free recording of all orders, the company can also only receive a delivery if there is an order. A wrong delivery is immediately recognized and rejected by the system. With the addition of best bidder analysis, this increases security for the procuring company as well as for its partner companies.

To handle these transactions, there will be eProcurement platforms, some of which already exist today, such as SAP's Ariba, which digitizes procurement right through to automated invoicing. This gives companies advantages in terms of conditions, security, and liquidity, while at the same time saving on personnel costs. It is no coincidence that procurement, of all things, is already partially digitized today with its knock-on effects in the company, because this is one of the best-defined operational functions.

The self-driving companies of 2035 will need cross-company eProcurement platforms with which the various ERP solutions can exchange information with each other smoothly and without loss. Intensive work is already being done on prototypes here, so significant leaps in development can be expected in the next few years. Assuming that the self-driving companies with their digital purchasing platforms work, it will subsequently depend on the reliability of the suppliers how well purchasing and subsequently all other operational functions are fulfilled. Thus the reliability of the partner enterprises will take on a particularly high value and will gain in relevance for procurement decisions.

Due to the high level of transparency across company boundaries, unreliable and technologically backward suppliers will therefore very quickly disappear from the market or be bought out by their competitors. This is because for the digital, self-driving company, a performance failure means a selective reversion to the analog system, so the problem must again be solved by people and by hand.

Here, the comparison with the self-driving car is obvious, where in an exceptional case, for which the vehicle is not programmed, humans do intervene and stop the vehicle or bring it back on track—even if the distant future lies in the complete mastery of all situations, both routine and exceptional. This is because humans also act in traffic with a high error rate. For example, practical experience shows that wrong-way drivers, when they realize that they are driving on the highway in the wrong direction, against the traffic, do not stop the vehicle or move to the side as they should. Due to their state of shock, they are not capable of making a decision. This means that they maintain their fatal behavior and continue driving at the same speed in the wrong lane in the wrong direction. A machine would recognize this mistake immediately and make the right decision without emotions, strictly rationally—or would not drive in the wrong direction in the first place.

While the error in the case of the wrong-way driver can have catastrophic consequences, making a mistake can, however, be useful in the sense of trial and error and provide the basis for new ideas. Where it makes sense, people should therefore continue to be allowed to make constructive mistakes; as already described, this is something they are particularly good at.

The corporate landscape will change structurally by 2035. The number of monopolists will increase, as will the number of niche providers. Either they have everything, like Amazon today—or they offer specialty products, making them difficult to replace and possibly allowing them to accept a limited degree of automation. Because of the significant investment required by a new software infrastructure, it will be larger companies that achieve preeminence in a particular industry and therefore take over many small companies that are technologically incapable keeping up. The second scenario, the use of niches developed by individual or several cooperating small suppliers, enables new forms of cooperation. These are facilitated due to increasing software-based capabilities. Depending on the particular order, a decision is made as to whether it can be handled alone or in association with cooperating partners.

The entire supply chain, from ordering to delivery of the finished product, will be fully digitized and automated by 2035. Even today, the purchase of many products activates an electronic account that provides a convenient overview of the current order, possible additional features, production and delivery status, or the delivery of spare parts. Similarly, billing is increasingly being done on a purely digital basis. For example, in the case of telecommunications companies, service is already provided and billed in a fully digitized manner; even the sending of the invoice PDF is based on a fully digitized process in which no human being has to intervene manually anymore.

All internal and external data are continuously recorded and processed in intelligent networks in line with the company's objectives. Political changes, natural disasters, raw material shortages or price fluctuations, for example, are also recorded and managed in an agile manner. Customer feedback is captured not only from complete data on the use of products and services, but also based on reactions in social media, and flows into the further design of the company's services, such as product design in terms of content or the calculation of future demand at all relevant locations. If there are disruptions in production, these are either eliminated automatically or a precise message is sent to the responsible experts, who receive the real-time status and possible interventions via an interactive user interface and can accordingly act quickly and accurately.

If there is a problem, a large part of the solution is thus dealt with via a multidivisional online platform. The human factor is provided for via the availability of chats or a telephone service hotline, although it should be noted that companies are endeavoring to further reduce the relative size of this factor. It is understandable that this human interaction, which is still desired in some areas, is made possible primarily in those areas where the margin is correspondingly high, in other words, in the case of high-priced products requiring explanation, in both the B2B and B2C areas.

6.3   Value Creation in the Self-Driving Organization

Value creation has several dimensions, and so there are different types. Basically, value creation can be understood as everything that helps to generate revenue, which in most companies—according to the "business model canvas" (Joyce & Paquin, 2016)—are the following:

- The unique selling proposition
- Key resources
- Key activities

Basically, every company generates a product. Whether that is a physical product or a service or a virtual product (such as a bank) is irrelevant in this context. A loan, for example, is a highly virtual product, because no money is transferred from the bank to the customer in physical form; instead, only certain rights and obligations are agreed upon—in the same way that an Amazon Prime subscription grants access rights to certain parties. By contrast, cars, beverages, and furniture will remain physical products, just as haircuts and physical therapy will remain services.

While physical products are charged for as finished work, services are usually charged according to the associated expenses, such as the time required and the cost of materials. Charging for virtual products is more complex and less transparent; here, there are basically no defined limits. Regardless of the category of product, the self-driving company must plan, track, and manage all services associated with the creation or manufacture of the product.

If you look at the industrial revolutions, they were always driven by the increase in value creation. The invention of the steam engine, for example, brought huge advances in logistics: Suddenly, machines took care of transportation. No longer were slow people or horse-drawn carts and oxcarts needed to struggle to transport steel parts or finished goods. In the course of the second industrial revolution, the triumph of machines in manufacturing prevailed, and factories were completely restructured on the basis of series production. Taylorism, inaugurating the scientific management of workflows, once again increased the value added and changed the conception of factories and its laborers. Each of the latter had his or her station on the assembly line and carried out the same manual operations there more and more efficiently. With digitization, the third industrial revolution ensured that not only physical activities but also mental activities were taken over by machines. In many cases, this led to the creation of new, monotonous activities, such as managers using Excel to perform the same evaluations over and over again.

Today, the fourth industrial revolution, Industry 4.0, is on the verge of once again increasing value creation by automating, in real time, coordinative and communicative processes that used to be handled slowly, and in an error-prone manner, by clerks or middle management. This again results in a significant acceleration of all processes, while at the same time creating considerable transparency within the company.

The self-driving company goes one step further and ensures that products are manufactured in a completely automated manner—transforming isolated, linear processes into holistically networked, multidimensional functions. The cost of manufacturing is based mainly on investments, made once, and ongoing energy and material costs, while personnel costs are drastically reduced.

So the driver of the fourth industrial revolution is primarily to improve value creation while reducing coordinating costs. Just as the steam locomotive, mass production, and providing employees with personal computers produced significant advances for those companies that were willing to invest in new technologies, those companies that tried to hold on to the old ways of doing things have disappeared, as documented, for example, by the death of the mills in the 1930s. Thus, it can also be assumed that the opportunities opened up by cognitive software will be drivers for the success of those companies that embrace these technologies and are willing to allow the corresponding changes in their enterprises.

One pioneer on the road to self-driving companies is Elon Musk. While the other car manufacturers adapted their production in part on the basis of completely outdated technologies, the Tesla manufacturer took a completely different path. He didn't want to build a factory, but to program one. The basic idea was simple: Once I have programmed something, it is subsequently very easy to change. The robotic systems used here are so flexible that they can support changes at any time. Elon Musk's success proves him right. His factories are capable of adapting to sharply rising sales, so they "scale" like a virtual Internet start-up, such as WhatsApp or TikTok. Based on this principle, Elon Musk can copy his gigafactory, initially built in Nevada starting in 2014, and set it up at any other suitable location or locations.

6.3.1 Research and Development

While value creation in self-driving companies will be highly automated, research and development of new products will continue to be a job for humans. However, this research and development will be driven by a wealth of information. This information will be provided in unprecedented quantity and quality from all areas of the company, customer channels, the Internet and all networked partner organizations.

People will continue to perform critical and commanding functions in this research and development process. However, based on data from all areas of the company, from production to customer behavior, simulations and modeling are now possible on the basis of artificial intelligence, which previously had to be created and produced in time-consuming manual work.

But beware: even Henry Ford recognized that good market research alone does not necessarily produce a good product. "If I had asked people what they wanted, they would have said faster horses!" So it's not just a matter of continuing a

6.3 Value Creation in the Self-Driving Organization

development in a linear fashion, but of creating completely new approaches and then trying out how well they are accepted by customers or with what effort they can be produced. The creative spark will therefore continue to come from people for some time to come, and will then be passed on to artificial intelligence, which in turn will create all simulations with unprecedented speed and quality. A recent example is the invention of the coffee capsule. The linear progression of existing technology would have been a further technical improvement of the fully automatic machine, incorporating even more mechanical elements and software to improve coffee quality, usability, maintenance, and cleaning. Instead, with the coffee capsule came a radical redefinition of the coffee-making process. The capsule maintains the aroma at the highest quality, the machine only needs to apply the necessary water pressure and is no longer contaminated by coffee residues, and maintenance and cleaning are easier than ever.

So in the future, it will continue to be up to humans to bring complex and hitherto elusive phenomena into these ideas, such as the "spirit of the times" or possible risk scenarios. Because he sometimes neglected to do this, industrial pioneer Henry Ford once also failed. In September 1957, he launched a new automobile product, the *Edsel*, which was developed on the basis of new ideas. With it, he introduced one of America's strangest cars, with a grille shaped like a horse collar—equated by people with a toilet seat—a "floating" speedometer that lit up when a certain speed was reached, and a cumbersome push-button transmission with controls attached to the hub of the steering wheel. The Edsel line was completely rejected by consumers. Though Ford expected to build 200,000 Edsels in the first year of production, only 63,000 ended up being made. Even with a quick revision completed in time for next year's model, the Edsel stumbled just a month after the vehicles were released. Likewise, things continued in the model's third year, and eventually the Edsel was phased out entirely. This example nicely illustrates that elaborate planning, lengthy market surveys, and significant investment of expertise do not always lead to the desired success of the product.

This rule will also apply in self-driving companies. Nevertheless, there will be product innovations and these will be developed in an evolutionary manner according to the "fail-fast" principle. In the self-driving company, countless parallel product ideas will be generated and followed up on. An early and rapid market launch is vital to this approach. Very early development stages of products are tested with individual customer groups. Numerous product variants are tested in parallel on different reference groups. This quickly provides a large database of feedback on the product and on individual variations. In the laboratory, this data can be evaluated and the ideal product variant can be designed. The "fail-fast" principle makes it possible to test different approaches, since they are not kept alive artificially. Only if the desired success is foreseeable is a product idea pursued further. All previous variants and ideas are quickly evaluated and then not pursued further.

6.3.2 Production Forecasting and Planning

With the targeted collection, analysis, and processing of market data, Michael Bloomberg became one of the richest people in the world, with a fortune of about $60 billion. The immeasurable value of his data for customers is based on the improved ability it gives them to plan their investment and production decisions by matching these analyses with the internal data or situation of their company.

Due to the faster pace of change in global markets, these data analyses will become more important in the years to come. While the process is still carried out by humans in most companies, for example by the CFO (the Chief Financial Officer) who subsequently discusses his or her analysis with the CEO, this process is becoming increasingly automated due to the potential provided by artificial intelligence and Big Data analytics. This subsequently provides a basis for planning that can be used to coordinate activities in production and in collaboration with suppliers. While purchasing and personnel decisions are still made today on the basis of diverse planning discussions and contract negotiations, in self-driving companies with overarching planning of sales and production, this can be done largely without human intervention.

One of the most important topics of focus in value creation in the coming years will be the prediction of future production. In addition to market data, sales planning and current sales figures must be incorporated into the forward-looking planning of production capacity. In companies of the past, this process would have been impossible due to siloed departments and disparate data pots. In self-driving companies, all company data are available to all concerned and to all software systems in the company. Sales processes are standardized and the data for them is available in digital form. This means that production can access the sales pipelines and their associated probabilities, and then schedule production capacities and inventories using intelligent algorithms. Idle capacity or fluctuations in production are detected at an early stage by these same intelligent algorithms and automatically mitigated by feedback loops back to sales.

6.3.3 Automation of Production

Not all core processes will change fundamentally in the course of artificial intelligence-based digitization. Thus, the way steel is produced will essentially continue to follow the tried and tested pattern—and a cow will best continue to eat fresh grass in order to grow up healthy. These forms of production will merely be supported and optimized by technology, especially if the production units are of a certain size. These scales can also be created by merging smaller production units, as is currently made possible, for example, for farmers through the "machinery ring" or similar collectives. Especially when you consider that a self-driving agricultural machine will cost several million euros and that a single farmer will no longer be able to afford such a machine. Nevertheless, the merger makes it possible to achieve a level of productivity that will keep these farmers competitive on the market.

6.3 Value Creation in the Self-Driving Organization

There will be exciting developments in the service sector: It can be assumed that some services will disappear completely from the market, while new ones will emerge. Cab drivers, who already have to fear for their existence due to competition from Uber, will have to look for new jobs in the next few years. The future of cabs and trucks lies in self-driving systems, which have already reached a high level of development at the current time and will soon surpass humans in terms of driving safety due to the dramatic increase in computer performance and the associated improvements in the field of artificial intelligence—the keyword here: pattern recognition. Self-driving cars will also possess other intelligent functions. Connected to the grid, they will choose the cheapest electricity provider themselves or feed in solar power from their owner's roof. After bringing their owner to the company in the morning, they will "work" as part of a passenger transport service, transporting other people. Thus, they do not "stand around" uselessly, but earn money for their owners. Humans will be providers of high-value empathic services in the personal transportation of the future. One scenario could be that people sit in the car as tour guides and tell the guests exciting stories about the city and its sights.

Many personal services will therefore continue to be provided by people in the future—and at a higher level than ever before. Other services will also change drastically. For example, there are already robots that cut people's hair. However, those who can afford it will continue to have their hair trimmed by their hairdresser while drinking a glass of Aperol and chatting about the new restaurant that has opened just around the corner. However, the costs for this will be multiple times higher than for automated services.

An exciting trend is the transformation from service to virtual product. In the past, we had to ask an expert if we wanted to know details about a certain topic—today, we take our cell phone, look it up on Wikipedia or watch a YouTube video if we can't manage to fold the stroller so that it fits in the trunk.

Physical products, on the other hand, are less likely to become virtual products. It can be assumed that only parts of these physical products will be virtualized or equipped with virtual services. Due to the comparatively cheap electric motor, which no longer consists of hundreds of complicated, small moving parts and transmission components that wear out, the physical product of the car will become cheaper and cheaper, while more and more intelligent software will be installed. This is exemplified today by the IQ Drive at Volkswagen, an intelligent driving assistance system that increases safety and comfort when driving. For example, it is already possible to control all functions by voice input, and turning knobs while driving will soon be a thing of the past—until the driver disappears altogether. The added value of the automobile will therefore be created increasingly by the software installed—partly because the production of the physical car of the future will become cheaper and cheaper as this production becomes fully automated.

6.3.4 Robotics and Digital Twins

While factories today use a large number of individual programmable robots, the future—as shown by the example of Elon Musk's gigafactory—will be the completely programmable factory. The physical work will be performed by standardized, highly flexible robots. Today, we primarily have the programmable robot arm, which is basically a good thing, but it is limited to a fixed location. Currently, people are the ones moving around the factory, in response to ongoing needs, and are increasingly supported by automated logistics systems.

The factory of the future will be continuously reconfigured and reprogrammed by algorithms to meet changing requirements. In this way, robots will constantly be deployed where they are needed at the moment. The instructions on how to carry out the individual work steps will also be automated, for example by means of digital twins.

The digital twin is the virtual copy of a physical object. The term was coined by Michael Grieves in 2002. He developed the principle of using virtual replication to achieve a new level of quality in automated production. Thus, digital twins are able to bridge the gap between the real and virtual worlds by capturing data from installed sensors on the real object in real time and connecting it to the virtual twin. The data from the "original" is evaluated and simulated in a virtual copy of the physical object. For example, the maintenance process on a machine is recorded and immediately digitized. The collected data can be stored either locally, in a decentralized way, or in a cloud. These digital twins will become irreplaceable in the further development of manufacturing, maintenance, and servicing processes. Ever more functions of the programmable factory will be based on the use of virtual replicas of the product, especially with the continuing increase in computing power.

Thus, communication and interaction between robots and humans will also be enabled on the basis of algorithms and Deep Learning and will be completely normal in 2035. As implemented by Volkswagen in its IQ Drive, many households in China already have assistance systems that can control automated home functions using simple voice input. Authorization takes place via voice recognition. Subsystems such as heating, cooling, shutters, ventilation, or vacuum cleaners are thus networked to form an intelligent home to which owners can communicate their current wishes and needs.

6.3.5 Automated Storage

Automated storage systems also function in principle like robots that perform specific work tasks. In an automated storage system, functions such as the storage, retrieval, and transfer of goods are carried out independently, and "commissioning" (the collecting of products for orders) is based on the "goods-to-man" principle. Automated conveyor technology guides the articles directly to the commissioner. In the future, this person will be a robot. Compared to traditional warehouses, automated storage systems have a number of advantages that contribute significantly

6.3 Value Creation in the Self-Driving Organization

to long-term cost reductions: they require less space, save energy, and shorten routes, as algorithms continuously calculate the most favorable overall solution. Other advantages include shorter access times and integrated material flow control.

Moreover, in the transition period to self-driving companies in 2035, warehouse automation will relieve warehouse employees of physically difficult and monotonous labor tasks—and the errors repeatedly made by humans will be reduced to a minimum. Automated warehouse management systems are based on robust and durable designs, dynamic and energy-efficient technology, and cloud-based warehouse management software that controls and manages all operations. The warehouse management system is central to controlling system inventory and managing material flow. It is therefore also referred to as the "warehouse's pacemaker."

In the self-driving company, the warehouse is fully connected to all other operational functions and there is continuous two-way real-time coordination, for instance, orders are triggered automatically, invoices are issued virtually, and all current data are available to controlling on the basis of the ongoing inventory, which in turn can be used to make decisions, such as negotiating new supply contracts with new partners.

The self-driving company thus knows exactly what was sold in the last period—ranging from the last year to the last quarter to the last second—and which demands are to be expected in the following period, knowledge it acquires by linking internal data with external data and forecasts. Depending on the wishes of management, information or warning messages can be set up on this basis in order to make any changes to the otherwise completely self-driving warehouse if reported data fall outside of the defined system parameters.

The example of automated logistics thus shows very well how the rigid boundaries within a company, as well as vis-à-vis the company's external environment, are broken down in a self-driving company, in favor of a hybrid overall organism that can be adapted in real time and is fully networked with all relevant actors. This interaction becomes even better the more that self-driving companies or organizations are involved—for example, the self-driving logistics company, which supplies the company with its current logistical and product-related delivery information, which the company then uses to adapt all processes to the new situation in service of the overall optimum.

Experiences in analog companies show that contrary to the overall optimum, parts of some companies always tend to strive only for the optimum of their department and thus actually worsen the overall result. This is due to deeply human emotions, blind ambition, profile neurosis, envy, resentment, career ambition, or narrow-mindedness. These impulses are often well known internally, and are the reason for conflicts, inadequate communication, and the withholding of valuable information. At best, there is a workshop once a year where some of this misconduct is uncovered, though 2 weeks later everything returns to the way it was.

6.4 Finance and Accounting and Corporate Management

The self-driving company will massively ease and reduce workload, especially in activities related to financial administration. Even today, modern ERP systems and the standardization of processes is laying the foundations. The following pages highlight the innovations made in the areas of accounting, financial transactions, and reporting.

In 2035 orders and invoices will be exchanged via a global contract or commercial platform. It will no longer be necessary to issue invoices and reenter them into an ERP system. The verification of purchase orders, contracts, and invoices will be fully automated. Payment transactions will be anchored directly in the ERP system, and there will be numerous payment transaction partners both inside and outside the company. The regional bank will no longer play a key role in payment transactions in this form. The choice of one's digital payment transaction partner will be decided on the basis of price per use case and global presence.

Under the heading of predictive forecasting, intelligent and automated simulation calculations will become established. Planning calculations will no longer be created manually by experts and others. The software system will take the figures from previous years and combine them with available market data. This will result in simulation values for a forecast, that is, a planning calculation.

Previously, it had taken weeks and months to prepare annual financial statements. The consistent digitization and integration of central ERP systems (even beyond company boundaries) enables the automated posting—in real time—of all documents, material flows, orders, investments, depreciation, and payments. This means that the financial situation of the company can be tracked at any time with the push of a button. The future will not bring real-time financial statements, but real-time reporting. Combining predictive forecasting with real-time accounting, it is possible to predict annual results with a high degree of accuracy at any time. So accounting and bookkeeping will change massively by 2030. Monthly reports, quarterly reports, and annual reports will be broken up. Any period (last week, 30 days, 90 days, 365 days) can be reported, key dates are no longer required, postings are made in real time and always correctly.

In 2020, all receipts still had to be entered manually into the system. A streetcar receipt for € 2.20, including VAT, had to be entered into the system by an employee and physically filed correctly. This monotonous work causes more costs than savings, even for a company in the highest tax bracket. For decades, this was hardly questioned, as people were so bogged down by grueling routines that it didn't even occur to them to question this nonsense on a higher, critical level. It was and still is even more annoying to have to call up careless customers when they do not deliver all of their receipts on time. We're not talking about minutes here, but hours that are senselessly wasted on unpleasant work, not to mention the annoyed customers. It costs the companies a lot of money, and it takes time from the employees' lives. And the careless customers don't get any better: they know that companies "always call back anyway if something's missing."

6.4 Finance and Accounting and Corporate Management

So it's time to take a new step in the evolution of companies and the people who work in them. Most companies are still largely analog. More and more companies are already more or less partially automated, especially in the area of web store retailers—even if customers have often not even noticed this yet. There is software that, thanks to artificial intelligence, now translates the web store into all languages very well and ever better. It also automatically optimizes search engine optimization and, if competition is high, the web store's ads as well. So once the store is planned, it can be active, with little effort, in national languages across the world. It is possible to sell the complete range of products to customers 7 days a week, 24 h a day, without the need for a field sales force and with minimal operating costs. Customers no longer need to be persuaded to buy a product that matches their interests, as they have already come to the store on their own. With the purchase, payment is made at the click of a button. The data and documents for the accounting system are also generated automatically.

An interesting aspect in connection with decisions are all the errors that occur, for example, due to unexpected changes in the environment. The self-driving company will function within the framework for which it is programmed, with as many exceptional situations as possible already integrated into the system, and it will learn from manual intervention. However, if an unexpected incident nevertheless occurs, the company will have to switch back to analog mode and humans will have to make the relevant decisions—with these decisions being prepared by algorithms based on comprehensive real-time data. A similar situation is conceivable when there is an unexpected deviation from target figures. For example, the management programs the company for 5% growth and receives timely feedback from the system that, based on the current data, this value can probably not be met. In parallel, simulations calculated by the algorithms come up with effects that cause different decisions. On this basis, the management can now make the desired decision and, given its sound data basis, communicate it very effectively to all relevant actors.

6.4.1 Interaction with the State and the Reinvention of Taxes

In the era of self-driving companies, laws will no longer be formulated exclusively in human language, but will additionally be implemented in and executed by software. Laws will be programmed into software algorithms (e.g., accounting systems, ERP) and these will be authorized by government agencies. These systems will calculate tax payments in real time and transfer them to the government. Manual processing or audits by external tax consultants will no longer be necessary. Audits will only take place at the level of system configurations and in the ERP system. Tax audits will also be carried out by the state on the basis of data from the ERP systems. Comparable systems already exist in the banking supervisory sector (Österreichische Nationalbank, 2020).

This circumstance will also fundamentally change the way people think by 2035. People who no longer compose, file, lose, misplace, search for again, stamp at some point, or sort documents manually will be freed up for a variety of cognitive activities that are of higher value both emotionally and socially. As a quick aside: with just 10 pieces of paper, there are 3,628,800 ways to put them in the wrong sequence or order, something easily verified by calculating 10 factorial. In the office of an average accountant there are thousands of receipts. It is easy to imagine the enormous potential of a networked system in which receipts are nothing more than data that is continuously collected and managed in real time. Even on weekends and at midnight, without extra pay.

The relevant tax laws are entered into the system once and subsequently always calculate the most favorable variant for the company. If all laws worldwide are online, digital search agents can also take care of this. Thanks to the continuously updated data, millions of variants can be checked in a very short time. If changes need to be made in other parts of the company as a result of these complex analyses, they can be continuously approved automatically within an authorized framework of predictive forecasting. Fundamental decisions are made by interdisciplinary teams that sit down and discuss them in terms of their long-term strategic significance, analyze risks and opportunities on the basis of future scenarios, develop ideas, and finally come to a decision.

Due to the continuous availability of all data, in 2035 the self-driving company could also pay its taxes in real time. There is also no longer any need for a tax advisor for routine tasks, as all current tax information is integrated the system. Likewise, the auditor will become superfluous, as these systems are completely transparent. The laws applied are no longer only in textual form, but are prepared as algorithms and are fed directly into the company, where they are mapped in the form of a computational core. Because this computational core works reliably and transparently, the tax office knows that all payments will be made correctly and in real time.

There will still be tax consultants in 2035, but they will mainly deal with fundamental, structural issues and act as business consultants. Of course, the businesses of the future will also strive to reduce their tax burden with imaginative constructs. Thus, even the profession of tax advisor will require a considerable amount of innovation and creativity. However, due to the complete transparency of these companies, the solutions come up with will be completely legal and will withstand all audits. This will also result in a psychological change. As game theory corroborates, the willingness to behave in accordance with the rules is considerably higher if we know that the other players are also doing so.

As a result, self-driving companies will also be "disruptive" to many other areas, such as public administration, which can be considerably simplified at all levels on this basis. It, too, can have access to all data in real time, and all decisions should be automated. Instead of official secrecy and printed files that are redacted, full transparency will prevail here as well, in that any query will be possible at any time on request.

The self-driving organization will permeate public administration at all political levels. Neither the EU nor the states of Germany, Austria, or Switzerland, nor the states and cantons that make them up, or their cities and municipalities can escape this development. The automated provision of administrative and other services and the self-service character of such services for citizens will be the focus of

6.4 Finance and Accounting and Corporate Management 109

development in the coming years. Once the transformation has been completed, all administrative processes will be digital, software-supported, and automated. However, some laws will still have to be legally adapted to this vision. The goal is to make legal adjustments that allow sovereign tasks to be automated. In this way, it will be possible for software to issue legally valid rulings and judgments.

Through unconditional, digital, and fully automated process management, employees in public administration are freed from administrative tasks and devote themselves to providing the best possible services for citizens and businesses. Software algorithms take over 80% of decision-making and support employees in their expertise and advisory function vis-à-vis political bodies.

Thanks to knowledge about citizens and their various phases in life, recurring and predictable administrative processes can be carried out automatically or early recommendations can be made. Information from citizens and businesses is collected once as part of the *once-only principle* and made available to all collaborating institutions. Digital interaction takes place via a one-stop service platform, with regional, analog offices remaining as service providers.

The organizational transformation of public administration will also be comparable to the development of self-driving vehicles. Here, too, the technical maturity of the "self-driving" administration, organization, or authority is differentiated on the basis of the autonomy levels that also serve as guidelines for autonomous driving vehicles. Constantly keeping the vision of the self-driving organization in focus, individual areas of an organization develop at different speeds. Based on the digitization and automation of organizational processes, 80% of all organizational decisions will eventually be made autonomously.

End-to-end management processes are being unconditionally replaced by automated software solutions. This means that manual entries, decisions, and approvals are no longer required. The service portfolio functions 100% digitally and without any human administrative work. These processes are "checked" once for legal compliance by the responsible officials. Thereafter they run fully automatically.

When advising and supporting political bodies, setting goals, and developing programs, complex issues and decision-making are involved. Under the principle of the self-driving organization, 80% of decisions will be made by software algorithms based on historical and extrapolated data and on the rules as defined by laws and regulations. All other decision-making processes are supported dynamically and transparently by the same systems.

Many administrative processes currently have to be completed at regular intervals (e.g., passport renewal) or can be predicted in advance (e.g., enrollment for family benefits). Due to the transparent availability of data, these processes can be fully automated and autonomous. As a result, there is no need for citizens to be present, service quality can be increased, and administrative overhead eliminated. Thanks to the information available about citizens and their various life stages, recommendations can be made for the administrative phases required, or services can be provided automatically.

In accordance with the once-only principle, information obtained from citizens and businesses is communicated only once to the administrative body and can then be reused by all areas of operations, service points, and collaborating institutions of the public sector. Autonomous actions can be taken here by means of software algorithms. The online portal provides citizens and businesses with easy access to all the services they need. In accordance with the one-stop service principle, all information on previous interactions with the administrative authority can be viewed with a single login and, in the few remaining cases in which applications are still required (such as registering for an event), one can apply online.

The transformation of countries, federal states, municipalities, and local bodies into digital, self-driving organizations can be seen as a central means of eliminating administrative workload. Due to the full automation of administrative tasks and autonomous decision-making, administrators are freed from tedious administrative processes and routine activities and can focus on their new core competence: interpersonal interaction.

Despite the digital handling of administration, regional service and the analog service points associated with it will remain intact. Trained employees specialize in providing content-related service advice and skills transfer so that citizens can act independently in the digital sphere. Digital, automated administration has less potential for error than manual processing and is also completely transparent. The shift to a digital, self-driving organization will thus lead to a rapid increase in efficiency and quality of service in the public sector, as well as an enormous reduction in costs. What it takes is the will to change. The resources used for this purpose will certainly be recouped due to the enormous, long-term savings it will generate.

6.4.2   A Day in the Life of a Manager in 2035

An ideal CEO or manager today plans a three-part day: he or she spends about a third of his/her time working for the employees who report to him/her, a third for customers, and a third for peer groups (predominantly in direct contact but also targeted reading and preparation of relevant information). In a typical 10-h day, the manager spends 3 h on customer-related activities, calls, regulations, and interventions. He or she spends another 3 h delegating, de-escalating, motivating, and representing, and another 3 h with shareholders and colleagues, exchanging ideas and discussing strategic and tactical considerations. The remaining hour is spent specifically and succinctly dealing with the most important correspondence.

Poor CEOs or managers are "email-driven" 70% of his/her daily work time: all actions are triggered frantically and at short notice due to constantly arriving messages. There is little time for cultivated, direct contact with the three stakeholder groups; due to this stressed state, this communication is not very effective and also makes a negative contribution to the working atmosphere as well as to customer satisfaction. In addition, there is a constant need to check whether instructions have been carried out, and in many cases hectic corrections are required. This type of manager will die out in the future. In the world of self-driving companies in 2035, there will no longer be a place for him.

In the future, charisma, competence, empathy, and creativity will be in demand, since operational and tactical decisions will be automated and it will no longer be necessary to check the extent to which an instruction has actually been implemented. Decisions will increasingly be simulated by the system in terms of their medium-term effects and are in this way improved and made easier. No longer are messages turned into gossip transmitted inaccurately, which then needs to be painstakingly reconstructed. This makes the manager much more effective. His head is freed up to think about fundamental strategic issues, the business's vision and mission, to discuss these with all relevant stakeholders, and to jointly develop creative approaches to solutions. Thus his/her overall activity profile will move more in the direction of generating added value for the company.

By being able to incorporate business environment data and Big Data, a wide range of simulations will become possible that seem unthinkable today, are currently still associated with a huge amount of effort, or can only be carried out by external consulting companies at high cost. In 2035, for example, it will be possible to analyze what effects the introduction of a 4-day week will have on the company, from the organization of work to tax and social security contributions to employee motivation, with the latter in turn flowing into productivity in the cyclical calculation model. If the decision is made in favor of the 4-day week, it is enough to program it into the human resources system. As a result, the entire corporate structure, from production to all contracts with employees and social security institutions, will be adjusted accordingly.

Managers will also encounter considerably less resistance, as the basis for all decisions will be completely comprehensible. Using a wide range of simulation tools, these decisions can be prepared in such a way that they can be made fully transparent for both shareholders and employees.

6.4.3 Leadership in the Self-Driving Organization

As described in Sect. 6.4.2, the executive in the self-driving organization thus ensures that all functions are largely automated and that the workforce can concentrate on higher tasks, such as developing ideas, and establishing and maintaining personal relationships with customers, suppliers, and stakeholders. Occasionally, it will be necessary to intervene manually in the event of breakdowns or other events that go beyond the range of the system's capabilities. Here, teams precisely based on the requirements of the situation will be formed, which take on this task with software support, for instance, if the company needs to move to another building. In contrast to the analogous organization, where all operational and tactical decisions are made by humans, the self-controlling organization can quickly resume regular operations after this intervention without management involvement. Compared to the analog organization, the intervention is also much faster, because even in this phase all the necessary information is available in real time. In the example of relocation, this would include all data on requirements for materials, workstations, and infrastructure, as well as automatically generated and requested tenders for missing resources or data regarding both actual and target requirements in the area of logistics.

6.5 Organization and Personnel

Organizations form a framework for a system in which resources are used to achieve the company's goals. In order for corporate objectives to be achieved, several resources are usually required, which then have to be coordinated. These resources include not only capital, equipment, and materials, but also people. In order for this system to function, a framework is needed that defines, coordinates, and oversees the tasks of those involved and thus reduces complexity. A company's success depends on how resources work together and how people, materials, capital, and technology are used. The decisive factor is how well organizations succeed in generating output through joint processing and thus in achieving an increase in value. The adaptability of organizations is decisive for their existence and success.

The unconditional alignment of the organization with the expectations of the market and its customers is what fuels the transformation to self-driving companies. The organizations of the future that create products and value will no longer be cut horizontally—in other words, there will no longer be a breach between organizational entities. In recent decades, classic organizations were often built up in service layers like multi-layer sandwiches. Today, this results in many losses due to internal friction and senseless trench warfare driven by power politics. In addition, there is a danger of disproportionate dominance by organizational entities that do not add value. The reason why people had previously introduced this service matrix organization was to leverage cost-synergy effects. For companies with a very high number of human employees, this form of organization was the most cost-efficient way to efficiently collaborate on value creation.

The self-driving organization, however, is oriented exclusively to the products it offers and will break down these classic service silo formations. This agile organizational design, headed by its product managers, is uncompromisingly aligned with the sellable product. Growth hacking, sales, value creation, purchasing, team management and delivery, and logistics are aligned with the products. Central software and controlling algorithms make it possible to turn the matrix organization upside down. At the center of the new silos is the product offered and its entire life cycle. In traditional organizations, there is a separate team for each task, so the holistic view and the vision for the product are missing. Through the transformation to interdisciplinary agile organizational forms, all these tasks are brought together in product teams. As automation advances and cognitive software solutions permeate all areas, significantly fewer people will be needed to manufacture and deliver products. These triggers and drivers will significantly change the collaboration model of the future. People will take center stage in self-driving companies, and the nature and content of

6.5 Organization and Personnel

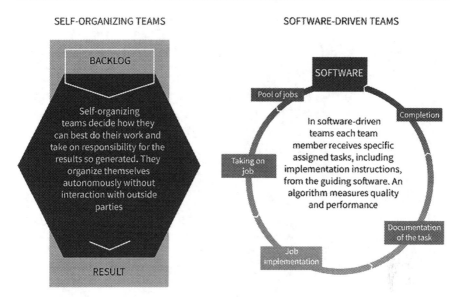

Fig. 6.4 Collaboration models in the self-driving company

their work will become of higher value. The structure of teams and the way they work will change radically.

In principle, collaboration between people will fall into two broad categories (see Fig. 6.4):

- Self-organizing teams: Self-organizing teams decide how best to do their work and take responsibility for the results to be produced. They organize themselves independently without interaction with outside parties.
- Software-driven teams: In software-driven teams, a governing software program assigns specific tasks, including implementation instructions, to each team member. Algorithms are used to measure quality and performance.

In the following sections, these two types of teams are described in greater detail.

6.5.1 Self-Organizing Teams

Self-driving organizations consist of countless decentralized, but self-organizing teams, which nevertheless work together in a concerted manner for a common goal. Intelligent and learning software systems take charge of the orchestration. These teams take an agile approach to their work and are unconditionally aligned with the needs of the market and their customers. The decisive factor here is that decisions and tasks are assigned and performed in a decentralized fashion. In this way, it is possible to react quickly and practically in real time to changes in customer

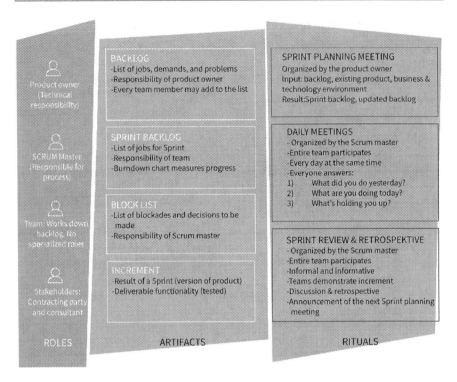

Fig. 6.5 Agile way of working with roles, artifacts and rituals

behavior or in capacity utilization. This is the greatest advantage of agile organizations.

In order for this decentralization to be successful, a framework is also needed, just as in classic organizational forms. *Scrum* is one of today's best-known and most widespread methods of agile management and an excellent basis for the design of self-organizing teams. The underlying structure is simple and the roles in the teams are clearly defined, making scrum quite easy to learn (cf. Fig. 6.5). There is a responsible specialist (the product owner) who defines the tasks, ranks them according to priorities, and makes changes if necessary. The team of employees works together with the process owner (Scrum master). Team composition and capacity utilization are reviewed on a regular basis. The team works through the customer and product requirements or tasks defined in the backlog (for example, in the case of repair and maintenance) in short iterations. During implementation, neither specialist nor process managers have any influence and the team acts completely autonomously. During recurring "sprints," feedback is given on the success of implementation and, on its basis, future project specification is generated.

The difference between the self-driving company in 2035 and the "classic" scrum is that the respective person in charge is presumably no longer a physical person, but an intelligent, self-teaching program that, as in the examples already described, learns on the basis of the feedback it receives and, in the process, becomes ever

6.5 Organization and Personnel

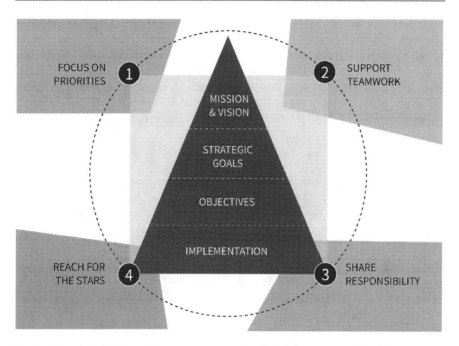

Fig. 6.6 Best practice for motivating control through objectives and key results (OKR)

better, ever more complex. For complex tasks such as strategy and management, customer interaction, and sales, a self-organized team will still consist of real people in 2035—because even in 2035 there will be no robots that can empathically build relationships with customers or deliver, unpack, assemble, and electrically wire a complicated machine in a customer company's industrial plant. Solving creative or novel individual activities and problems, as well as devising new products for new human needs, will be the job of self-organizing teams.

The team thus shares a pool of digital work and chooses its tasks independently. When, where, and how is decided by the team as a team effort. For example, in the future a maintenance team will continue to be responsible for an operating plant, but the nature of the work will change. The team's task will increasingly be to adapt the algorithms used to the new situation. Instead of the classic skilled worker, there will be a need for a knowledge worker. When the machine generates an error message, the team itself will determine how the maintenance system is to be upgraded. There is an actively usable stock of knowledge for this purpose.

There are already sensible management methods for these decentralized, self-organizing teams. *Objectives and key results* (OKRs) is a framework for modern management that links the individual tasks of teams and employees with corporate strategy, plans, and vision (see Fig. 6.6). OKRs are objective in nature and can be viewed by the entire company. Through these methods, the self-organizing teams can be directed by management in a motivating way. In contrast to *management by objectives*, the objectives are not assigned top-down, but are broken down independently by the respective level for its own team. This process starts with company-wide objectives and key results and is individually defined by each level and team for its own area of responsibility.

A number of best practices have emerged from day-to-day consulting activities using this methodology. For example, OKRs are not used for the obligatory management of self-organizing teams. However, they can be used to increase motivation. The management and coordination of all agile and self-organizing teams in a company can only be achieved by centralized and networked software systems. The transformation and introduction of this management method in large companies takes 3–5 years and only then leads to improved performance. This increase in efficiency will only set in if all processes are radically automated. In the negative case, employees perceive the new organizational form as more complex manually and administratively than classic organizational forms. For this reason, the most important ingredient for agile organizations is the unconditional automation of administrative.

6.5.2 Software-Driven Teams

Software-driven teams share a digital work pool and a software program distributes tasks autonomously. The call center represents an older version of software-driven teams: employees proceed to their workstations and the system independently dials one number after the other; as soon as one call is ended, the system dials the next person to be contacted. This is also a good example of the need we have to talk to people when we have specific concerns. Everyone knows and hates the computer-generated answering systems that play the same tune over and over again at the push of buttons 1, 2, or 3 and, in the worst case, brutally terminate your call after making you wait for 15 minutes. People still prefer to communicate with other people, especially when it comes to personal and private matters. In 2035, people will still talk to other people wherever this is desired and makes sense.

Software-driven teams will get their goals and the results they require through a pool of jobs that is software managed. The software does the distributing of these jobs. For example, it tells employee Stefan Meier to go to customer Müller Limited at 10:00 a.m. and service the milling machine there. For this, Stefan Meier receives precise instructions explaining the individual steps of the repair. Pictures and 3D simulations are used to explain exactly how to calibrate the rotation axis, for example. Stefan Meier must have a certain basic skill in handling tools and using measuring equipment, as well as a keen grasp of human nature. However, it is no longer necessary to know every machine and all the conceivable repairs associated with it by heart. This information is provided by the self-driving company. So a human being will continue to replace the broken bolt in the future—only he or she will be greatly assisted by an intelligent, self-learning system. He/She no longer has to be fully "trained on the machine" by an experienced colleague.

In principle, these are activities that machines cannot perform automatically and autonomously, such as empathic communication with customers, care-giving activities, manual repairs, and programming activities to rectify errors. The planning, implementation, and quality assurance of these activities, which are not fully automated, are carried out independently by the people involved. This is referred to as a software-driven team. The software checks quality automatically through feedback from subsequent processors, customers, or partners.

In the long term, it can be assumed that software-driven teams will become increasingly rare as more and more of their activities are taken over by machines, even if it is not always possible to predict in advance how exactly this will take place. In the 1950s, for example, there was a vision of a human-like robot washing the dishes, vacuuming, and mowing the lawn. Things turned out differently: the dishwasher has been in use for many years, and small intelligent machines clean the carpet and cut the grass at regular intervals—all without the need for arms or legs. However, we will probably continue to tidy up the kitchen ourselves for a while longer—or our children will if they have been raised right.

6.5.3 Matching and the Hunt for Key Workers

A key factor in the success of self-driving companies is attracting the right key workers. This activity also needs to be highly digitized, then automated, and finally performed by intelligent algorithms. The fact that algorithms are being used for recruiting processes is, in principle, nothing new. As early as 2009, the German Federal Employment Agency built an algorithm for placing job seekers in Germany that was able to match individual qualification profiles or job preferences with the existing supply, up to and including active notification of the respective person as soon as a suitable job became available in his or her field. This has made it possible to automate a considerable part of the work of employment agents. Previously this job had been highly time consuming and demanded the painstaking matching of many individual parameters such as age, education, work experience, gender, and job preferences. Despite the new technology, though, personal consultation still took place. However, because the new system reduces overall workload, this consultation can be conducted at a qualitatively higher level. In addition, the more than 100,000 consultants are just a mouse click away from accessing any and all relevant job offers. All in all, the system generated savings of several billion euros annually, mainly because people were unemployed for a shorter period of time—so the several hundred million euros spent on the new placement and counseling information system quickly paid for itself.

The matching processes just described will continue to develop considerably in the coming decades and will be used in a wide variety of professional and private applications. Searching and being found via social media platforms such as XING or LinkedIn is already widespread today. Our entire professional history is stored there and confirmed by our work colleagues and our superiors. Companies are also increasingly posting their current job offers online. Instead of submitting elaborate letters of application to these offers, interested parties need only click to send off their own profiles.

In the era of the self-driving company, the job market will be divided into members of self-organizing teams and members of software-driven teams. Recruiting team members for the latter will not be costly because the matching just discussed will be software-driven. As soon as someone is willing to work, a suitable job offer will be made to him or her. In self-driving companies, individual, isolated tasks will increasingly have to be performed. The vision is that instead of permanent employment, these tasks will be assigned to the best person available. After completion of this isolated task, payment will be made and the employment relationship dissolved. Both sides will benefit from this arrangement. Due to the efficient allocation of isolated tasks, there will always be work for those looking for it. Their monthly earnings will be significantly higher than what people are used to today, and the desired activity can be freely chosen and will be more in line with their own interests. It will be worthwhile for companies as they will always get the best specialist for the job in question.

The highly qualified key workers for self-organizing teams have to be recruited individually and at great expense. Companies will actively approach these key workers. Although software will be used both to scout the labor market and to select and approach individual candidates, the classic recruitment interview and the actual hiring will always be carried out by individuals. Loosely in line with the basic proposition: people want to work for people, not for algorithms.

References

Joyce, A., & Paquin, R. L. (2016). The triple layered business model canvas: A tool to design more sustainable business models. *Journal of Cleaner Production, 135*, 1474–1486.

Österreichische Nationalbank. (2020). *Integrated reporting data model*. https://www.oenb.at/en/reporting/integrated-reporting-data-model.html. English version accessed on 17 February 2023.

Humans and the Self-Driving Organization

7

The primary motivation behind my vision of the self-driving company is to empower people in businesses and organizations. People need to be freed from technically nonsensical and endlessly boring repetitive work. People should be employed according to their passion and their abilities and in this way find enjoyment in their work. Repetitive and highly analytical work must be done by software algorithms because software makes fewer mistakes and does not grow tired and apathetic. Finally, work must be financially rewarding for each and every employee—and, on the flip side, businesses must be highly efficient and profitable in order to succeed internationally in a multipolar world. Only then can they pay above-average compensation for valuable human labor.

It would be a fallacy to think that this technological revolution can be stopped by means of regulations and laws. History teaches us that we have never been able to stop technological progress in our history, nor have we ever wanted to. Jobs were destroyed only to be completely reinvented a few years and decades later. Blood- and sweat-inducing tasks were turned into activities of human interaction in air-conditioned and heated office spaces. In the next 15 years, we will see a similar transformation of the human workforce. Our focus will be on creative and empathic activities. Software will guide us in this and we will perceive it as a source of support.

Already today, the majority of managers are governed by the software in their calendars. Statements such as "The appointment was not in the calendar, so I was not on site" confirm this thesis. This chapter looks at the self-driving company from the perspective of employees. The different effects on the life cycle in the company, the daily work routine, and the legal framework are described on the basis of different roles.

© The Author(s), under exclusive license to Springer-Verlag GmbH, DE, part of Springer Nature 2023
F. Schnitzhofer, *The Self-Driving Company*, Future of Business and Finance, https://doi.org/10.1007/978-3-662-68148-0_7

7.1 Six Theses on the Role of Humans in Companies in 2035

The vision of the self-driving company may throw many readers off guard and stir up fears or prejudices. In fact, however, it shows us what is essential. The companies of the future will continue to be run for and by humans like us. Software algorithms will only ever perform tasks that direct and implement.

As we delve deeper into the vision of self-driving companies, the following theses about the role of people in these organizations emerge:

1. People want to buy products from people.
2. People want to be advised by people.
3. People want to buy goods manufactured by people.
4. People want to work with people.
5. People want to spend time with people.
6. People will always have jobs.

Currently, it is cheaper to have a machine make the goods because human labor is subject to very high taxation. So the problem, as well as its solution, is based primarily on a framework set by politics. If people are to be able to afford services provided by people, the taxation of human labor must be eliminated.

Self-driving companies will produce goods automatically, and this will be done more cost-effectively than ever before. Companies or end consumers will be able to buy these products particularly cheaply in the future. As a result, these goods will be available to a very broad segment of society.

However, there will continue to be a demand for personal services and high-quality handcrafted products. A new tax framework will make it possible for these services to be affordable. So there will continue to be a market for the handmade. In 2035, consumers will still be willing to spend significantly more money on a handmade sandwich. One example of this that can already be seen comes from the fast food sector. Automated production will further reduce the unit costs of burgers, which, together with the higher quality of the ingredients, will result in a better and healthier product at the same consumer price.

In addition, product complexity will continue to increase. This development provides for a countervailing trend in prices. This means that falling unit costs will be partly offset by this added value. This creates benefits on both sides: On the company side, profit margins and productivity increase, and on the customer side, benefits increase. There are already examples of this today. Robotics, for example, provides vacuum cleaners and lawn mowers that can be manufactured inexpensively, that can precisely measure even the most complicated surfaces of their owners, and that thus provide their services in a highly individualized manner. Drones, home automation, autonomous vehicles, and entire smart cities are already capable of comparable services. For people's quality of life, then, these developments mean an overall greater variety of better yet affordable products.

7.2 An Example of Defensiveness: The Self-Driving Train

Technological progress is not always met with the appropriate energy. The self-driving car in private transportation is a vision that can already be implemented in the foreseeable future. Self-driving public transportation, on the other hand, is already a reality, as shown by the example of Shenzhen in China (see Sect. 2.8). One part of this is the self-driving train. The fact that the self-driving train was not implemented in Europe long ago is hardly comprehensible in logical terms and can rather be explained by political inadequacy and lack of will. The operation of such a train is considerably simpler than that of a car. The timetable, route, speeds, and all stops are clearly predefined. Changes due to road works, wind breakage of trees, and other obstructions can be quickly entered into the overall system, resulting in a recalculation of the timetables, which in turn is communicated to the trains' operating systems.

A self-driving train could be safer than a human-operated one because a computer does not fatigue. If a suicidal person jumps onto the tracks, the human can't brake in time either—moreover, the computer doesn't suffer trauma that often results in several months of incapacity and psychotherapy. It would be much easier to erect fences along the route—there is no sensible reason why this has not yet been done, because wildlife crossing could be ensured with other corridors, superstructures, or underpasses.

So it seems to be purely a matter of will (or lack thereof) on the part of the public administration that these measures were not implemented long ago. The argument that the return on investment cannot be calculated should not be invoked either. Ultimately, it is a matter of technological leadership and a realistic time frame. This is more likely to be 15 years rather than two to five. The self-driving train is thus a good example for illustrating how much potential that already exists today thanks to automation and artificial intelligence is not being recognized or exploited—or even worse: is not being exploited because people simply don't want to.

7.3 Employees and Their Life Cycle in the Self-Driving Organization

While the life cycle of employees in the traditional company today still involves a considerable amount of human labor, in the self-driving company a large part of all subfunctions and administrative tasks will be accomplished intelligently and automatically. The overriding goal of any interaction, however, is mutual well-being; it's about getting the right, motivated people for the jobs who will enjoy doing their tasks. These people must be constantly developed and their work situation must respond and be adapted dynamically to any change in their personal situation. At the end of the joint life cycle, a smooth and resource-saving transition to a new phase of life—for instance, retirement or change of company—must be made possible.

This life cycle already starts with the automatic identification of recruiting needs based on internal company data. The system knows in good time when a person is leaving the company or when new people are needed due to the kickoff of a major project. The algorithms ensure an exact determination of qualitative and quantitative requirements. These needs are used to generate profiles that trigger automated recruiting of employees, which takes place primarily via social media, since this is where most people publish their profiles according to their skills, but also according to their needs and interests.

From a technical perspective, specific platforms are used for the following tasks:

- Role definition
- Definition of skill set and desired outcome
- Addressing of potential candidates
- Communication and matching
- Negotiation or bidding competition
- Hiring or rejection

If a given task was completed or if the person performed well during his/her period of employment, a quality certificate is created based on the data, which is used to upgrade the applicant's profile for further tasks.

So there will still be employees in the future, but their relative numbers will decline—on the one hand, because people's need for security will have largely been met via basic (income) security, and on the other hand, because it takes considerably less effort with algorithms to recruit personnel for special tasks in a results-oriented manner. The improved matching makes these jobs highly attractive—the low cost of automated manufacturing frees up more resources for a high level of compensation, which is highly performance-oriented due to the high level of transparency. In addition, jobs will entail more personal responsibility.

Promotions will also be automated and intelligent, capturing not only employee performance data but also their wants and needs. Based on this data, large parts of personnel and organizational development will take place, such as building, informing, and motivating teams, surveying training needs, planning continuing education and training, and, of course, internal matching should there be changes in internal needs.

Giving notice will be less emotionally charged than it currently is. This is due to the following:

- The role of employment will be devalued and replaced by a variety of attractive models.
- The better networking of people across company boundaries will reduce frictional unemployment and shorten unwanted "periods of idleness" considerably.
- The wide range of telecommuting and translation options will overcome regional boundaries, an effect that was already becoming apparent in 2020 based on the surge in office work done at home.
- As a result, termination becomes part of a new beginning, for example, when a development project is successfully completed and the employee responsible is

7.3 Employees and Their Life Cycle in the Self-Driving Organization

awarded a certificate that allows him or her to take another step on one of the new career ladders.

The self-driving company serves as an attractive employer for everyone working at the company. The implications this will have for the different roles in the self-driving organization are presented in the coming sections.

7.3.1 The Role of Leadership

Top managers and owners will be relieved of many pseudo-decisions due to the high degree of self-direction. The extreme transparency of the company, coupled with the possibilities of obtaining all desired information on the status quo in all respects—liquidity, capacity utilization, order situation, structure of markets or customers, clear forecasts and simulations based on reliable, complex data—increases the degree of freedom enjoyed by this group. Their work will be reduced to far-reaching strategic decisions that will be based on excellent data. In addition, planning horizons will shift massively. Strategies will be designed for periods of more than 10 years. The goal for this group is to balance a profitable and competitive company with more leisure time and quality of life despite great responsibility.

7.3.2 The Role of Management

The roles of middle management will shift toward building and maintaining relationships and toward creativity as the day-to-day small decisions are handled by the self-learning algorithms. The algorithm will handle these decisions better than humans in many areas because of the unlimited resources available to handle complex, real-time data sets. In addition, computers will work day and night and over the weekend without tiring or getting sick. Percentage-wise, a large number of management jobs will be rendered obsolete by self-driving companies.

The job profile of managers will therefore be qualitatively upgraded, tiring routines will be eliminated, and there will be more interpersonal contact in order to coordinate and agree on new tasks and to find creative solutions that go beyond the capabilities of IT. Due to the increased agility of companies, the dissolution of the classic hierarchical organizational structure and thus also of vertical and horizontal departmental boundaries, these personal contacts will be strongly task-related. Agility thus brings about significantly greater diversity, with managers working with different people in equally self-organizing teams. The important skills of managers will be to be empathetic to the group, to approach each other with openness, curiosity and interest, to listen actively, and to be able to discuss ideas at a highly sophisticated and differentiated level. Managers are understood more as coaches, counselors, and trainers. They will bring the necessary basic knowledge to their actions and interactions; further information will be available on request in a variety of forms from internal and external data sources, and can be prepared in a targeted manner with easy-to-use tools. The need and expediency of direct management responsibility will fade into the background. Direct personnel responsibility will be administered by the software algorithms and self-organizing teams will need no external command: they need people who motivate and lead by example.

7.3.3 The Role of Knowledge Workers

Knowledge workers and subject matter experts also operate at the interface with managers, especially when the acquisition and preparation of data is beyond the scope of the latter. Thanks to the multiplicity of devices—smartphones, tablets, notebooks—and online data storage, this work can be done anywhere. In principle, the work of knowledge workers is location-independent and in 2035 the legal framework will also have been adapted accordingly. It will be possible for them to work anywhere. Nevertheless, companies will provide modern office facilities so that knowledge workers can meet and organize themselves in the self-organizing teams envisaged. Of course, technology is omnipresent here, and international team members or people working from home can be invited to meetings online and actively participate in those meetings. Video conferencing systems, interactive whiteboards, and an unlimited number of cameras and microphones enable a hybrid online and face-to-face meeting. It's not work location and attendance that are relevant, but results.

Retaining the group of knowledge workers will become increasingly more important for the company. In addition to the self-explanatory diversity of the team and gender equality, this group of employees will be granted numerous privileges. They will have a completely flexible working time model that, above all, adapts to the different needs in the individual's life. For example, the desire for a demanding workload will be highest shortly after completing one's education and lowest at the birth of one's offspring or at the end of one's working life. The self-driving companies will plan for and organize these cycles for each person in the company. A spontaneous wedding including a year off—because of subsequent world travel—is not an unsolvable problem for agile corporate structures. On the contrary, this means of gaining creativity and broadening horizons will be seen as positive further development by one's colleagues.

The skills of knowledge workers include a willingness to learn and the ability to understand algorithms and data and subsequently transform information into insights. These insights must in turn be programmed into the software systems.

7.3.4 The Role of Workers

The insights from Sect. 6.5 on self-organizing and software-driven teams are the basis for the understanding of the role and everyday life of workers in self-driving companies. Their activities are supported to a high degree by software.

The "foremen" of the self-organizing teams receive their jobs from the software in their backlog and coordinate internally on how to work together on them. The activity itself is also supported by continuously available real-time data. Time and again, certain tasks are performed jointly with robots or digital twins. The state of completion of the task, its performance, and its quality are recorded by the control system.

For the workers, the transition to software-driven teams is fluid. In the "extreme case," the members of the software-driven team complete their diverse, ever-changing tasks with the support of precise instructions prepared by algorithms. An example of this is replacing a component in a highly automated storage system because the software has calculated that it is at the end of its service life—or changing the blades of an autonomous lawn mower. The instructions generated for these tasks are presented in a highly visual, animated, and linguistically comprehensible manner.

7.3.5 The Role of Auxiliary Workers

The role of auxiliary workers will change dramatically in self-driving companies. For the most part, they will no longer be in a static employment relationship with a company. They will be matched with companies via online platforms—similar to social media—for individual isolated tasks. The future will show whether they will be hired and placed solely through staffing companies, or whether direct task-related employment relationships will also develop through these task placement platforms. This will require some dusting off of labor law in Europe, as people are currently being pushed into self-employment. The employment model would be comparable to seasonal employment, but the activity interval might be reduced to weeks, months, or days.

The auxiliary workers enter their application profile, personal preferences, and formal skills and education into the platform's database. The software then automatically adds all tasks that are accepted and supplements them with the evaluation of the individual made by the assigning companies. Conversely, the auxiliary worker can also evaluate the company. This creates a task-oriented ecosystem that provides sufficient human resources for tasks arising from software-driven teams.

For those working in this system, task-oriented job placement means constantly changing and exciting activities. People and their preferences are in the foreground and there is a freedom of choice never known before. In times when high levels of capital are required, for instance, when building one's house, people are more likely to look for activities with high pay. This could be simple work at the blast furnace or night repair work on the railroad track or the highway. While raising children, one will reduce activity and additionally choose tasks that can be done remotely if necessary, such as simple troubleshooting programming, manual remote control of robotic systems, or identifying patterns to teach neuronal networks. Thus, the decision about the extent of employment is always up to the coworker.

7.4 Who "Is" the Self-Driving Company?

As has been shown, the control of the self-driving company is automated to a high degree. The question therefore arises as to who is the self-driving company: Is it the managers or the workforce? The answer is that it is the owner who represents the company, either alone or together with the shareholders. The self-driving company will serve the owner or this group of people; in doing so, it will generate profit, create jobs, provide the public sector with tax money, and thus ensure general prosperity due to the favorable profit forecast resulting from considerably increased productivity.

On this basis, the company can also fulfill its social duties by offering its coworkers security and attractive areas of work. Due to the favorable long-term cost effects, coworkers will be paid exceptionally well with comparatively short working hours.

The roles of owners and managing directors will merge more closely, because it will be easier to direct the company thanks to transparency and ongoing high-quality forecasts. There will be no need to attend ten meetings a day in 80-h weeks when much of the operational and tactical decision-making is fully automated. As a result, the self-driving company will provide prosperity for its managers and owners, and give them greater freedom and quality of life. Of course, those who want to can work more and earn even more; this freedom of choice will also be available.

7.5 The Self-Driving Company: By People for People

As has been shown in the previous chapters with scores of examples and details, the self-driving company is an attractive vision that offers a wide range of benefits for all involved. It frees us as coworkers from paralyzing, repetitive routines and ensures that we can develop our true potential and contribute according to our stage of life and the wishes associated with it. As customers, our needs will be better understood than ever, and it will be easier than ever to get exactly what we want. Our products will be better and more sustainable, thanks to the enormous resources freed up in companies. Those companies that have sought to resist this development will have long since closed down, leaving only first-class small niche suppliers to enrich the market with their high-quality, handcrafted products.

As owners and managers, we no longer have to slave away for 70 h a week—as we did in the 2020s. No longer do we have to deal with annoying controls, a flood of emails, and constant personnel conflicts. This is ensured by the entire organism's unified, clear focus on common goals and being freed from constant small-scale operational decisions.

In the coming years, the idea of self-driving companies will evolve from being an idea in economic science and will pervade our politics, society, and legislation. Many frameworks will be geared towards these highly automated organisms of the future. Society as a whole will benefit from highly efficient tax-paying companies and coworkers, more than offsetting the transitional effects for those disadvantaged by this transformation. Life will be more livable for people in a society with humanitarian self-driving companies, and our work activities more humane.

Now it is up to us to see that this progress is real progress in the sense of designing humane companies for a better world. However, the many insights in this book give us hope that this will be achieved. Above all, the absolute transparency of self-driving companies towards customers, coworkers, the state, and society will increasingly ensure that all forces are bundled in the right direction.

Printed in the United States
by Baker & Taylor Publisher Services